Daily Strength for Daily Needs

Compiled by
Mary Tileston

Whitaker House

Unless otherwise indicated, all Scripture quotations are taken from the *King James Version* (KJV) of the Bible.

DAILY STRENGTH FOR DAILY NEEDS

ISBN: 0-88368-472-1
Printed in the United States of America
Copyright © 1997 by Whitaker House

Whitaker House
30 Hunt Valley Circle
New Kensington, PA 15068

2 3 4 5 6 7 8 9 10 11 12 13 / 06 05 04 03 02 01 00 99 98 97

January 1

They go from strength to strength. —Psalm 84:7

First the blade, then the ear, after that the full corn in the ear. —Mark 4:28

Build thee more stately mansions, O my soul,
      As the swift seasons roll!
      Leave thy low-vaulted past!
Let each new temple, nobler than the last,
Shut thee from heaven with a dome more vast,
      And thou at length art free,
Leaving thine outgrown shell by life's unresting sea!

                    Oliver Wendell Holmes

*H*igh hearts are never go for long without hearing some new call, some distant voice of God, even in their dreams. Soon they are observed to break up the camp of ease and start on some fresh march of faithful service. And, looking higher still, we find those who never wait until their moral work accumulates, and who reward resolution with no rest. Therefore, with them the alternation is instantaneous and constant. They do the good only to see the better, and see the better only to achieve it. They are too meek for transport, too faithful for remorse, too earnest for repose. Their worship is action, and their action is ceaseless aspiration.

                    James Martineau

*The LORD shall preserve thy going out and thy coming
in from this time forth, and even for evermore.*
—Psalm 121:8

*LORD, thou hast been our dwelling place in all
generations.* —Psalm 90:1

With grateful hearts the past we own;
The future, all to us unknown,
We to Thy guardian care commit,
And peaceful leave before Thy feet.

Philip Doddridge

*W*e are like Him with whom there is no past or
future, with whom a day is as a thousand
years, and a thousand years as one day, when we do
our work in the great present. We then are leaving
both past and future to Him to whom they are ever
present. We then fear nothing, because He is in our
future as much as He is in our past, as much as, and
far more than, we can feel Him to be in our present.
Being partakers then of the divine nature, resting in
that perfect All-in-all in whom our nature is eternal
too, we walk without fear, full of hope and courage
and strength to do His will. We wait for the endless
good that He is always giving as fast as He can
make us able to take it in.

George MacDonald

January 3

As thy days, so shall thy strength be.
—Deuteronomy 33:25

Sufficient unto the day is the evil thereof.
—Matthew 6:34

Oh, ask not thou, How shall I bear
   The burden of tomorrow?
Sufficient for today, its care,
   Its evil and its sorrow;
God imparteth by the way
Strength sufficient for the day.

Jane Euphemia Saxby

*H*e who has so many causes of joy, and so great, is very much in love with sorrow and irritability if he loses all these pleasures and chooses to sit down upon his little handful of thorns. Enjoy the blessings of this day, if God sends them, and bear patiently and sweetly the evils of it, for this day only is ours. We are dead to yesterday, and we are not yet born to tomorrow. But if we look abroad and bring into one day's thoughts the evil of many things certain and uncertain, what will be and what will never be, our load will be as intolerable as it is unreasonable.

Jeremy Taylor

January 4

Let not sin therefore reign in your mortal body, that ye
should obey it in the lusts thereof. Neither yield ye your
members as instruments of unrighteousness unto sin:
but yield yourselves unto God, as those that are alive
from the dead, and your members as instruments of
righteousness unto God. For sin shall not have domin-
ion over you: for ye are not under the law, but under
grace. —Romans 6:12–14

Oh, empty us of self, the world, and sin,
And then in all Thy fulness enter in;
Take full possession, Lord, and let each thought
Into obedience unto Thee be brought;
Thine is the power, and Thine the will, that we
Be wholly sanctified, O Lord, to Thee.

C. E. J.

*E*xamine steadily some one sin, which seems to
stand out before you, in order to root out every
fiber of it by God's grace. Purpose strongly, by the
grace and strength of God, wholly to sacrifice this
sin or sinful inclination to the love of God, not to
spare it, until you leave none of it remaining, neither root nor branch.

Not only root out this sin by God's help, but
allow yourself to gain, by that same help, the opposite grace. If you are tempted to be angry, try hard,
by God's grace, to be very meek; if you are proud,
seek to be very humble.

Edward B. Pusey

*That he might present it to himself a glorious church,
not having spot, or wrinkle, or any such thing; but that
it should be holy and without blemish.*
—Ephesians 5:27

Ye also, as lively stones, are built up a spiritual house.
—1 Peter 2:5

One holy Church of God appears
Through every age and race,
Unwasted by the lapse of years,
Unchanged by changing place.

Samuel Longfellow

*T*here has been a temple upon the earth, a spiritual temple, made up of living stones. There is a temple composed of souls, a temple with God for its light, and Christ for the high priest, with wings of angels for its arches, with saints and teachers for its pillars, and with worshippers for its pavement. Wherever there is faith and love, this temple is.

Cardinal John Henry Newman

To whatever worlds He carries our souls when they will pass out of these imprisoning bodies, in those worlds these souls of ours will find themselves part of the same great temple, for it belongs not to this earth alone. There can be no end of the universe where God is, to which that growing temple does not reach. It is the temple of a creation to be wrought at last into a perfect utterance of God by a perfect obedience to God.

Phillips Brooks

January 6

For God giveth to a man that is good in his sight wisdom. —Ecclesiastes 2:26

Meanwhile with every son and saint of Thine
　　Along the glorious line,
Sitting by turns beneath Thy sacred feet
　　We'll hold communion sweet,
Know them by look and voice, and thank them all
　　For helping us in thrall,
For words of hope, and bright examples given
To shew through moonless skies that there is light in heaven.

John Keble

*I*f we cannot live at once and alone with Him, we may at least live with those who have lived with Him and find, in our admiring love for their purity, their truth, and their goodness, an intercession with His pity on our behalf. To study the lives, to meditate the sorrows, to commune with the thoughts, of the great and holy men and women of this rich world is a sacred discipline. This discipline deserves at least to rank as the forecourt of the temple of true worship and may train the tastes before we pass the very gate of heaven. We forfeit the chief source of dignity and sweetness in life, next to direct communion with God, if we do not seek converse with the greater minds that have left their marks on the world.

James Martineau

Do not think it wasted time to submit yourself to any influence that may bring upon you any noble feeling.

John Ruskin

January 7

*The exceeding greatness of his power to us-ward who
believe, according to the working of his mighty power.*
—Ephesians 1:19

The lives which seem so poor, so low,
  The hearts which are so cramped and dull,
The baffled hopes, the impulse slow,
  Thou takest, touchest all, and lo!
They blossom to the beautiful.

Susan Coolidge

A root set in the finest soil, in the best climate,
and blessed with all that sun and air and rain
can do for it, is not so sure of its growth to perfection as every man may be, whose spirit aspires after
all that God is ready and infinitely desirous to give
him. For the sun does not meet the springing bud
that stretches towards it with half that certainty
that God, the source of all good, communicates
Himself to the soul who longs to partake of Him.

William Law

If we stand in the opening of the present moment with all the length and breadth of our faculties
unselfishly adjusted to what it reveals, we are in the
best condition to receive what God is always ready
to communicate.

Thomas Cogswell Upham

January 8

As we have therefore opportunity, let us do good unto all men. —Galatians 6:10

Let brotherly love continue. —Hebrews 13:1

> I ask Thee for a thoughtful love,
> Through constant watching wise,
> To meet the glad with joyful smiles,
> And to wipe the weeping eyes,
> And a heart at leisure from itself,
> To soothe and sympathize.
>
> Anna Laetitia Waring

*S*urely no one is so full of cares, or so poor in gifts, that to him, waiting patiently and trustfully on God for His daily commands, He will not also give direct opportunities for serving Him, increasing according to his strength and desire. There is so much to be set right in the world, there are so many to be led and helped and comforted, that we must continually come in contact with such in our daily lives. Let us only take care that, by the glance being turned inward or strained onward or lost in vacant reverie, we do not miss our turn of service, and pass by those to whom we might have been sent on an errand straight from God.

Elizabeth Charles

Look up and not down; look forward and not back; look out and not in; and lend a hand.

Edward Everett Hale

January 9

*And in every work that he began in the service of the
house of God, and in the law, and in the commandments, to seek his God, he did it with all his heart, and
prospered.* —2 Chronicles 31:21

*What shall we do, that we might work the works of
God?* —John 6:28

Give me within the work which calls today,
   To see Thy finger gently beckoning on;
So struggle grows to freedom, work to play,
   And toils begun from Thee to Thee are done.
              James Freeman Clarke

God is a kind Father. He sets us all in the places
where He wishes us to be employed, and that
employment is truly our *"Father's business"* (Luke
2:49). He chooses work for every person, which will
be delightful to him, if he does it simply and humbly. He always gives us strength enough, and sense
enough, for what He wants us to do. If we either tire
ourselves or puzzle ourselves, it is our own fault.
And we may always be sure, whatever we are doing,
that we cannot be pleasing Him if we are not happy
ourselves.

              John Ruskin

Because thy lovingkindness is better than life, my lips shall praise thee. —Psalm 63:3

Whosoever shall seek to save his life shall lose it; and whosoever shall lose his life shall preserve it.
—Luke 17:33

O LORD! my best desires fulfill,
　　And help me to resign
Life, health, and comfort, to Thy will,
　　And make Thy pleasure mine.

William Cowper

What do our heavy hearts prove but that other things are sweeter to us than His will? That we have not attained to the full mastery of our true freedom, the full perception of its power? That our sonship is yet but faintly realized, and its blessedness not yet proved and known? Our consent would turn all our trials into obedience. By consenting we make them our own and offer them with ourselves again to Him.

Cardinal Henry Edward Manning

Nothing is intolerable that is necessary. Now God has bound your trouble upon you, with a design to try you, and with purposes to reward and crown you. You cannot break these cords; therefore, lie down gently and allow the hand of God to do what He pleases.

Jeremy Taylor

January 11

I will be glad and rejoice in thy mercy: for thou hast considered my trouble; thou hast known my soul in adversities. —Psalm 31:7

Nay, all by Thee is ordered, chosen, planned—
Each drop that fills my daily cup; Thy hand
Prescribes for ills none else can understand.
      All, all is known to Thee.
                Adelaide Leaper Newton

God knows us through and through. Not even the most secret thought, which we most hide from ourselves, is hidden from Him. As we come to know ourselves through and through, we come to see ourselves more as God sees us. Then we catch some little glimpse of His designs with us, how each ordering of His providence, each check to our desires, each failure of our hopes, is just fitted for us, and for something in our own spiritual state, which others do not know of, and which, until then, we did not know. Until we come to this knowledge, we must take all in faith, believing in the goodness of God towards us. As we know ourselves, we, thus far, know God.

                Edward B. Pusey

Let the words of my mouth, and the meditation of my heart, be acceptable in thy sight, O LORD, my strength, and my redeemer. —Psalm 19:14

The thoughts that in our hearts keep place,
   Lord, make a holy, heavenly throng,
And steep in innocence and grace
   The issue of each guarded tongue.
Thomas Hornblower Gill

*T*here is another kind of silence to be cultivated, besides that of the tongue regarding others. I mean silence regarding oneself—restraining the imagination, not permitting it to dwell too much on what we have heard or said, not indulging in the fantastic scenes of picture thoughts, whether of the past or future. Be sure that you have made much progress in the spiritual life when you can control your imagination, so as to fix it on the duty and occupation actually existing, to the exclusion of the crowd of thoughts which are perpetually sweeping across the mind. No doubt, you cannot prevent those thoughts from arising, but you can prevent yourself from dwelling on them. You can put them aside. You can check the self-complacency or irritation or earthly longings that feed them. By the practice of such control of your thoughts, you will attain that spirit of inward silence which draws the soul into a close communion with God.
Jean Nicolas Grou

Speak not evil one of another, brethren. —James 4:11

Let all bitterness, and wrath, and anger, and clamour, and evil speaking, be put away from you, with all malice. —Ephesians 4:31

> If aught good thou canst not say
>   Of thy brother, foe, or friend,
> Take thou, then, the silent way,
>   Lest in word thou shouldst offend.
>
> Anonymous

*I*f there is any person to whom you feel dislike, that is the person of whom you ought never to speak.

Richard Cecil

To recognize with delight all high and generous and beautiful actions, to find a joy even in seeing the good qualities of your bitterest opponents, and to admire those qualities even in those with whom you have the least sympathy, this is the only spirit that can heal the love of slander.

Frederick William Robertson

Thy servants are ready to do whatsoever my lord the king shall appoint. —2 Samuel 15:15

I love to think that God appoints
My portion day by day;
Events of life are in His hand,
And I would only say,
Appoint them in Thine own good time,
And in Thine own best way.

Anna Laetitia Waring

If we are really and always and equally ready to do whatever the King appoints, all the trials and irritations arising from any change in His appointments, great or small, simply do not exist. If He appoints me to work there, will I lament that I am not to work here? If He appoints me to work indoors today, am I to be annoyed because I am not to work outdoors? If I meant to write His messages this morning, will I grumble because He sends interrupting visitors, rich or poor, to whom I am to speak, or show kindness for His sake, or at least obey His command, *"Be courteous"* (1 Pet. 3:8)? If all of myself is really at His disposal, why should I be put out if today's appointment is some simple work for my hands or errands for my feet, instead of some seemingly more important doing of head or tongue?

Frances Ridley Havergal

January 15

For this is the will of God, even your sanctification.
—1 Thessalonians 4:3

> Between us and Thyself remove
> Whatever hindrances may be,
> That so our inmost heart may prove
> A holy temple, meet for Thee.
> Latin Manuscript of 15th Century

Seek, in the presence of God, to know yourself. Then seek to know for what God sent you into the world, how you have fulfilled it. Are you yet what God willed you to be? What yet do you lack? What is God's will for you now? What thing can you now do, by His grace, to obtain His favor and approve yourself unto Him? Say to Him, *"Teach me to do thy will; for thou art my God"* (Ps. 143:10), and He will say unto your soul, "Fear not; I am your salvation." He will speak peace unto your soul. He will set you in the way. He will bear you above things of sense, and praise of men, and things that perish in your grasp, and give you, if but afar off, some glimpse of His own, unfading, unsetting, unperishing brightness and bliss and love.

Edward B. Pusey

January 16

Now our Lord Jesus Christ himself, and God, even our Father, which hath loved us, and hath given us everlasting consolation and good hope through grace, comfort your hearts, and stablish you in every good word and work. —2 Thessalonians 2:16–17

> When sorrow all our heart would ask,
> We need not shun our daily task,
> And hide ourselves for calm;
> The herbs we seek to heal our woe
> Familiar by our pathway grow,
> Our common air is balm.
>
> John Keble

Oh, when we turn away from some duty or some fellow creature, saying that our hearts are too sick and sore with some great yearning of our own, we may often sever the line on which a divine message was coming to us. We shut out the man, and we shut out the angel who had sent him on to open the door. There is a plan working in our lives, and if we keep our hearts quiet and our eyes open, it all works together. If we don't, it all fights together and goes on fighting until it comes right, somehow, somewhere.

Annie Keary

*Beloved, think it not strange concerning the fiery trial
which is to try you, as though some strange thing
happened unto you: but rejoice, inasmuch as ye are
partakers of Christ's sufferings.* —1 Peter 4:12–13

We take with solemn thankfulness
Our burden up, nor ask it less,
And count it joy that even we
May suffer, serve, or wait for Thee,
Whose will be done!

John Greenleaf Whittier

eceive every inward and outward trouble. Receive every disappointment, pain, uneasiness, temptation, darkness, and desolation, with both your hands as a true opportunity and blessed occasion of dying to self and entering into a fuller fellowship with your self-denying, suffering Savior. Look at no inward or outward trouble in any other view. Reject every other thought about it, and then every kind of trial and distress will become the blessed day of your prosperity. That state is best which exercises the highest faith in, and fullest resignation to, God.

William Law

*Thou shalt rejoice in every good thing which the LORD
thy God hath given unto thee.* —Deuteronomy 26:11

Rejoice evermore...In every thing give thanks.
—1 Thessalonians 5:16, 18

Grave on thy heart each past "red-letter day"!
Forget not all the sunshine of the way
By which the Lord hath led thee; answered prayers,
And joys unasked, strange blessings, lifted cares,
Grand promise-echoes! Thus thy life shall be
One record of His love and faithfulness to thee.

Frances Ridley Havergal

Gratitude is maintained in a watchful, minute attention to the particulars of our state, and to the
multitude of God's gifts, taken one by one. It fills us
with a consciousness that God loves and cares for us,
even to the least event and smallest need of life. It is
a blessed thought that from our childhood God has
been laying His fatherly hands upon us, and always
in benediction, that even the strokes of His hands are
blessings and among the chiefest we have ever received. When this feeling is awakened, the heart
beats with a pulse of thankfulness. Every gift has its
return of praise. It awakens an unceasing daily discourse with our Father—He speaking to us by the
descent of blessings, we to Him by the ascent of
thanksgiving. And all our whole lives are thereby
drawn under the light of His countenance and are
filled with a gladness, serenity, and peace which only
thankful hearts can know.

Cardinal Henry Edward Manning

January 19

Let the heart of them rejoice that seek the LORD.
— Psalm 105:3

The joy of the LORD is your strength. — Nehemiah 8:10

Be Thou my Sun, my selfishness destroy,
Thy atmosphere of Love be all my joy;
Thy Presence be my sunshine ever bright,
My soul the little mote that lives but in Thy light.

Gerhard Tersteegen

I do not know when I have had happier times in my soul than when I have been sitting at work with nothing before me but a candle and a white cloth, and hearing no sound but that of my own breath, with God in my soul and heaven in my eye. I rejoice in being exactly what I am—a creature capable of loving God and who, as long as God lives, must be happy. I get up and look for a while out of the window, and gaze at the moon and stars, the work of an almighty hand. I think of the grandeur of the universe, and then sit down, and think myself one of the happiest beings in it.

A Poor Methodist Woman, 18th Century

The LORD taketh pleasure in his people: he will beautify
the meek with salvation. —Psalm 149:4

> Send down Thy likeness from above,
> And let this my adorning be:
> Clothe me with wisdom, patience, love,
> With lowliness and purity.
>
> Joachim Lange

*W*ith what divine lines and lights the exercise of godliness and charity will mold and gild the hardest and coldest countenance, or to what darkness their departure will consign the loveliest! It cannot be explained in words. For there is no virtue the exercise of which, even momentarily, will not impress a new fairness upon the features. The moral and intellectual faculties have operation not on the features only, but on the whole body, for all the movements and gestures, however slight, are different in their modes according to the mind that governs them. And on the gentleness and decision of right feeling follows grace of actions and, through continuance of this, grace of form.

John Ruskin

There is no beautifier of complexion or form or behavior like the wish to scatter joy and not pain around us.

Ralph Waldo Emerson

Even the youths shall faint and be weary, and the young men shall utterly fall: but they that wait upon the LORD shall renew their strength; they shall mount up with wings as eagles; they shall run, and not be weary; and they shall walk, and not faint. —Isaiah 40:30–31

> Lord, with what courage and delight
>   I do each thing,
> When Thy least breath sustains my wing!
>   I shine and move
>   Like those above,
>   And, with much gladness
>   Quitting sadness,
> Make me fair days of every night.
>
> Henry Vaughan

*M*an, by living wholly in submission to the Divine Influence, becomes surrounded with, and creates for himself, internal pleasures infinitely greater than any he can otherwise attain to. It is a state of heavenly beatitude.

James Pierrepoint Greaves

By persisting in a habit of self-denial, we will, beyond what I can express, increase the inward powers of the mind, and will produce that cheerfulness and greatness of spirit that will fit us for all good purposes. We will not have lost pleasure but changed it—the soul being then filled with its own intrinsic pleasures.

Henry More

Then shall we know, if we follow on to know the LORD.
—Hosea 6:3

And, as the path of duty is made plain,
May grace be given that I may walk therein,
    Not like the hireling, for his selfish gain,
With backward glances and reluctant tread,
Making a merit of his coward dread,
    But, cheerful, in the light around me thrown,
    Walking as one to pleasant service led;
    Doing God's will as if it were my own,
Yet trusting not in mine, but in His strength alone!

John Greenleaf Whittier

*I*t is by doing our duty that we learn to do it. As
long as men dispute whether or not a thing is
their duty, they never get the nearer. Let them set
ever so weakly about doing it, and the face of things
alters. They find in themselves strength that they
did not know of. Difficulties, which it seemed to
them they could not get over, disappear. For He ac-
companies our action with the influences of His
blessed Spirit, and each performance opens our
minds for larger inpourings of His grace and places
them in communion with Him.

Edward B. Pusey

That which is called considering what is our
duty in a particular case, is very often nothing but
endeavoring to explain it away.

Bishop Joseph Butler

*If thou draw out thy soul to the hungry, and satisfy the
afflicted soul; then shall thy light rise in obscurity, and
thy darkness be as the noon day: and the LORD shall
guide thee continually.* —Isaiah 58:10–11

If thou hast Yesterday thy duty done,
    And thereby cleared firm footing for Today,
Whatever clouds make dark Tomorrow's sun,
    Thou shalt not miss thy solitary way.
Johann Wolfgang von Goethe

O Lord, You who are our Guide even unto death,
grant us, I pray You, grace to follow You wherever You go. In little daily duties to which You call
us, bow down our wills to simple obedience, patience
under pain or provocation, strict truthfulness of
word and manner, humility, and kindness. In great
acts of duty or perfection, if You should call us to
them, uplift us to self-sacrifice, heroic courage, laying down of life for Your truth's sake or for a
brother. Amen.
Christina G. Rossetti

January 24

I will bless the LORD, who hath given me counsel.
—Psalm 16:7

*Not slothful in business; fervent in spirit; serving the
Lord.* —Romans 12:11

Mine be the reverent, listening love
That waits all day on Thee,
With the service of a watchful heart
Which no one else can see.

Anna Laetitia Waring

Nothing is small or great in God's sight. Whatever He wills becomes great to us, however seemingly trifling, and if once the voice of conscience tells us that He requires anything of us, we have no right to measure its importance. On the other hand, whatever He would not have us do, however important we may think it, is as nothing to us. Now do you know what you may lose by neglecting this duty, which you think so trifling, or the blessing that its faithful performance may bring? Be sure that if you do your very best in that which is laid upon you daily, you will not be left without sufficient help when some weightier occasion arises. Give yourself to Him, trust Him, fix your eyes upon Him, listen to His voice, and then go on bravely and cheerfully.

Jean Nicolas Grou

If ye know these things, happy are ye if ye do them.
—John 13:17

Therefore to him that knoweth to do good, and doeth it not, to him it is sin. —James 4:17

> We cannot kindle when we will
>   The fire that in the heart resides,
> The spirit bloweth and is still,
>   In mystery our soul abides:
> But tasks in hours of insight willed
> Can be through hours of gloom fulfilled.
>
> Matthew Arnold

*D*eep-rooted customs, though wrong, are not easily altered. But it is the duty of all to be firm in that which they certainly know is right for them.

John Woolman

Do not hurt your conscience with any known sin.
Samuel Rutherford

He who does not do a certain thing often acts unjustly, not only he who does a certain thing.
Marcus Aurelius Antoninus

Every duty we omit obscures some truth we should have known.

John Ruskin

O the depth of the riches both of the wisdom and knowledge of God! how unsearchable are his judgments, and his ways past finding out! —Romans 11:33

It doth not yet appear what we shall be. —1 John 3:2

No star is ever lost we once have seen,
We always may be what we might have been.
Since Good, though only thought, has life and breath,
God's life—can always be redeemed from death;
And evil, in its nature, is decay,
And any hour can blot it all away;
The hopes that lost in some far distance seem,
May be the truer life, and this the dream.

Adelaide Anne Procter

St. Bernard has said, "Man, if you desire a noble and holy life, and unceasingly pray to God for it, if you continue constant in this your desire, it will be granted unto you without fail, even if only in the day or hour of your death. And if God should not give it to you then, you will find it in Him in eternity. Of this be assured." Therefore, do not relinquish your desire, though it is not fulfilled immediately, or though you may swerve from your aspirations or even forget them for a time. The love and aspiration that once really existed live forever before God, and in Him you will find the fruit of it. That is, to all eternity it will be better for you than if you had never felt them.

John Tauler

For thus saith the high and lofty One that inhabiteth eternity, whose name is Holy; I dwell in the high and holy place, with him also that is of a contrite and humble spirit, to revive the spirit of the humble, and to revive the heart of the contrite ones. —Isaiah 57:15

> Without an end or bound
> Thy life lies all outspread in light;
> Our lives feel Thy life all around,
> Making our weakness strong, our darkness bright;
> Yet is it neither wilderness nor sea,
> But the calm gladness of a full eternity.
>
> Frederick William Faber

O Truth, You who are Eternity! And Love, You who are Truth! And Eternity, You who are Love! You are my God. To You do I cry night and day. When I first knew You, You lifted me up, so that I might see there was something for me to see, and that I was not yet where I could see. And You, streaming forth Your beams of light upon me most strongly, did beat back the weakness of my sight, and I trembled with love and awe. And I perceived myself to be far off from You in the region of unlikeness.

St. Augustine

*O fear the LORD, ye his saints: for there is no want to
them that fear him.* —Psalm 34:9

*Thou openest thine hand, and satisfiest the desire of
every living thing.* —Psalm 145:16

What Thou shalt today provide,
　Let me as a child receive;
What tomorrow may betide,
　Calmly to Thy wisdom leave.
'T is enough that Thou wilt care;
Why should I the burden bear?

John Newton

*H*ave we found that anxiety about possible consequences increased the clearness of our
judgment and made us wiser and braver in meeting
the present and arming ourselves for the future? We
should pray for this day's bread and leave the next
to itself. We should not huddle our days together.
We should allot to each day its appointed task, not
deferring it to the future, and drawing upon the future for its troubles, which must be met when they
come whether we have anticipated them or not.
Then we will find a simplicity and honesty in our
lives, a capacity for work, an enjoyment in it, to
which we are now, for the most part, strangers.

John Frederick Denison Maurice

January 29

I the LORD...*will hold thy right hand, saying unto thee, Fear not; I will help thee.* —Isaiah 41:13

Show thy marvellous lovingkindness, O thou that savest by thy right hand them which put their trust in thee.
—Psalm 17:7

> I take Thy hand, and fears grow still;
> Behold Thy face, and doubts remove;
> Who would not yield his wavering will
> To perfect Truth and boundless Love?
>
> Samuel Johnson

*D*o not look forward to the changes and chances of this life in fear; rather look to them with full hope that, as they arise, God, whose you are, will deliver you out of them. He has kept you up to this time. Hold fast to His dear hand, and He will lead you safely through all things. And, when you cannot stand, He will bear you in His arms. Do not look forward to what may happen tomorrow. The same everlasting Father who cares for you today will take care of you tomorrow and every day. Either He will shield you from suffering, or He will give you unfailing strength to bear it. Be at peace then, and put aside all anxious thoughts and imaginations.

Francis de Sales

If I take the wings of the morning, and dwell in the uttermost parts of the sea; even there shall thy hand lead me, and thy right hand shall hold me.
—Psalm 139:9–10

I cannot lose Thee! Still in Thee abiding,
    The end is clear, how wide soe'er I roam;
The Hand that holds the worlds my steps is guiding,
    And I must rest at last in Thee, my home.

Eliza Scudder

How can we come to perceive this direct leading of God? By looking carefully within yourself and abiding within the gates of your own soul. Therefore, let a man be at home in his own heart and cease from his restless chase of, and search after, outward things. If he is thus at home while on earth, he will surely come to see what there is to do "at home"—what God commands him inwardly without means, and also outwardly by the help of means. Then let him surrender himself and follow God along whatever path his loving Lord thinks fit to lead him. Whether it is to contemplation or action, to usefulness or enjoyment; whether in sorrow or in joy, let him follow on. And if God does not cause him to feel His hand in all things, let him still simply yield himself up and go without, for God's sake, out of love. Let him still press forward.

John Tauler

In all thy ways acknowledge him, and he shall direct thy paths. —Proverbs 3:6

He leadeth me. —Psalm 23:2

In "pastures green"? Not always; sometimes He
Who knoweth best, in kindness leadeth me
In weary ways, where heavy shadows be.

So, whether on the hilltops high and fair
I dwell, or in the sunless valleys, where
The shadows lie, what matter? He is there.

Henry H. Barry

*T*he Shepherd knows what pastures are best for His sheep, and they must not question or doubt but trustingly follow Him. Perhaps He sees that the best pastures for some of us are to be found in the midst of opposition or earthly trials. If He leads you there, you may be sure they are green for you, and you will grow and be made strong by feeding there. Perhaps He sees that the best waters for you to walk beside will be raging waves of trouble and sorrow. If this should be the case, He will make them still waters for you, and you must go and lie down beside them and let them have all their blessed influences upon you.

Hannah Whitall Smith

February 1

Now the God of patience and consolation grant you to be likeminded one toward another according to Christ Jesus. —Romans 15:5

Let patience have her perfect work. —James 1:4

Make me patient, kind, and gentle,
    Day by day;
Teach me how to live more nearly
    As I pray.

Sharpe's Magazine

*T*he exercise of patience involves a continual practice of the presence of God, for we may be called upon at any moment for an almost heroic display of good temper. And it is a short road to unselfishness, for nothing is left to self. All that seems to belong most intimately to self, to be self's private property, such as time, home, and rest, are invaded by these continual trials of patience. The family is full of such opportunities.

Frederick William Faber

Now we exhort you, brethren, warn them that are unruly, comfort the feebleminded, support the weak, be patient toward all men. —1 Thessalonians 5:14

The little worries which we meet each day
May lie as stumbling blocks across our way,
Or we may make them steppingstones to be
    Of grace, O Lord, to Thee.

Anna E. Hamilton

*W*e must be continually sacrificing our own wills, as opportunity serves, to the wills of others. We must be bearing, without notice, sights and sounds that annoy us. We should be setting about this or that task, when we would much rather be doing something very different. We need to be persevering in it often, when we are thoroughly tired of it. We must keep company for duty's sake, when it would be a great joy to us to be by ourselves. We must do this despite all the trifling inconvenient accidents of life, despite bodily pain and weakness long continued and perplexing us often when it does not amount to illness. We need to do this even when losing what we value and missing what we desire. We should not let disappointment in other people, or willfulness, unkindness, ingratitude, or folly, in cases where we least expect it, hinder us from sacrificing our wills.

John Keble

February 3

*Search me, O God, and know my heart: try me, and
know my thoughts: and see if there be any wicked way
in me, and lead me in the way everlasting.*
—Psalm 139:23–24

Save us from the evil tongue,
From the heart that thinketh wrong,
From the sins, whate'er they be,
That divide the soul from Thee.

Anonymous

*W*hatever your habitual thoughts are, the same
also will be the character of your mind, for
the soul is dyed by the thoughts. Dye it then with a
continuous series of such thoughts as this: that
where a man can live, there he can also live well. If
he must live in a palace, then he can also live well in
a palace.

Marcus Aurelius Antoninus

Imagine a person who sets himself to the task
of steadily watching his thoughts for one hour, at-
tempting to preserve his mind in a simple, humble,
healthful condition. Will he not speedily find that
his emotions are multiform, self-reflecting, and self-
admiring emotions? They are like locusts ready to
eat up every green thing in his land. Will he not
then discern in himself a state as much opposed to
simplicity and humility as night is to day?

Mary Anne Kelty

February 4

If any man offend not in word, the same is a perfect man, and able also to bridle the whole body.
—James 3:2

Set a watch, O LORD, before my mouth; keep the door of my lips. —Psalm 141:3

What! never speak one evil word,
    Or rash, or idle, or unkind!
Oh, how shall I, most gracious Lord,
    This mark of true perfection find?
Charles Wesley

How hard a thing it is from day to day to meet our fellowmen, our neighbors, or even our own households, in all moods, all disagreements between the world outside us and the frames within, all states of health, of anxiety, of preoccupation; and show no signs of impatience, ungentleness, or inattentive self-absorption. How difficult it is to do this with only kindly feeling finding expression, and unfriendly feeling at least inwardly imprisoned. When we remember our temptations to give quick indulgence to disappointment or irritation or unsympathizing weariness, we will be ready to acknowledge that the man who has attained this is master of himself. And this man, in the graciousness of his power, is fashioned upon the style of a perfect man.
John Hamilton Thom

Blessed are they that keep judgment, and he that doeth righteousness at all times. —Psalm 106:3

For then shalt thou lift up thy face without spot; yea, thou shalt be stedfast, and shalt not fear: because thou shalt forget thy misery, and remember it as waters that pass away. —Job 11:15–16

> In the bitter waves of woe,
>   Beaten and tossed about
> By the sullen winds that blow
>   From the desolate shores of doubt,
> Where the anchors that faith has cast
>   Are dragging in the gale,
> I am quietly holding fast
>   To the things that cannot fail.
>
> Washington Gladden

*I*n the darkest hour through which a human soul can pass, whatever else is doubtful, this at least is certain: If there is no God and no future state, yet, even then, it is better to be generous than selfish, better to be chaste than licentious, better to be true than false, better to be brave than a coward. Blessed beyond all earthly blessedness is the man who, in the tempestuous darkness of the soul, has dared to hold fast to these venerable landmarks. Thrice blessed is he, who, when all is dreary and cheerless within and without, when his teachers terrify him, and when his friends shrink from him, has obstinately clung to moral good. Thrice blessed, because his night will pass into clear, bright day.

Frederick William Robertson

February 6

Whoso putteth his trust in the LORD shall be safe.
— Proverbs 29:25

I will cry unto God most high; unto God that performeth all things for me. — Psalm 57:2

Only thy restless heart keep still,
    And wait in cheerful hope; content
To take whate'er His gracious will,
    His all-discerning love hath sent;
Nor doubt our inmost wants are known
    To Him who chose us for His own.

Georg Neumarck

God has brought us into this time. He has done this, and not ourselves or some dark demon. If we are not fit to cope with that which He has prepared for us, we would have been utterly unfit for any condition that we imagine for ourselves. In this time we are to live and wrestle, and in no other. Let us humbly, tremblingly, bravely look at it, and we will not wish that the sun could go back its ten degrees, or that we could go back with it. If easy times are departed, it is so that the difficult times may make us more in earnest, that they may teach us not to depend upon ourselves. If easy belief is impossible, it is so that we may learn what belief is, and in whom it is to be placed.

John Frederick Denison Maurice

February 7

Obey my voice, and I will be your God, and ye shall be my people: and walk ye in all the ways that I have commanded you, that it may be well unto you.
—Jeremiah 7:23

And oft, when in my heart was heard
Thy timely mandate, I deferred
The task, in smoother walks to stray;
But thee I now would serve more strictly, if I may.
William Wordsworth

*P*ray to Him to give you what Scripture calls *"an honest and good heart"* (Luke 8:15) or *"a perfect heart"* (2 Kings 20:3), and, without waiting, begin at once to obey Him with the best heart you have. Any obedience is better than none. You have to seek His face. Obedience is the only way of seeing Him. All your duties are obediences. To do what He bids is to obey Him, and to obey Him is to approach Him. Every act of obedience is an approach. It is an approach to Him who is not far off, though He seems so, but close behind this visible screen of things that hide Him from us.

Cardinal John Henry Newman

As soon as we lay ourselves entirely at His feet, we have enough light given to us to guide our own steps. We are like the foot soldier, who hears nothing of the councils that determine the course of the great battle he is in, but hears plainly enough the word of command that he must himself obey.

George Eliot

February 8

He leadeth me beside the still waters. He restoreth my soul: he leadeth me in the paths of righteousness for his name's sake. —Psalm 23:2–3

> He leads me where the waters glide,
> The waters soft and still,
> And homeward He will gently guide
> My wandering heart and will.

John Keble

Out of obedience and devotion arises a habitual faith, which makes Him, though unseen, a part of all our lives. He will guide us in a sure path, though it will be a rough one. Though shadows hang upon it, He will be with us. He will bring us home at last. It may be through much trial and weariness, in much fear and fainting of heart, in much sadness and loneliness, in griefs that the world never knows, and under burdens that the nearest never suspect. Yet He will suffice for all. By His eye or by His voice, He will guide us, if we are docile and gentle; by His staff and by His rod, if we wander or are willful. By any way, and by all means, He will bring us to His rest.

Cardinal Henry Edward Manning

February 9

And I was afraid, and went and hid thy talent in the earth: lo, there thou hast that is thine. —Matthew 25:25

> Time was, I shrank from what was right,
> From fear of what was wrong;
> I would not brave the sacred fight,
> Because the foe was strong.
>
> But now I cast that finer sense
> And sorer shame aside;
> Such dread of sin was indolence,
> Such aim at heaven was pride.
> Cardinal John Henry Newman

*I*f someone falls into some error, he does not fret over it, but rising up with a humble spirit, he goes on his way rejoicing anew. Were he to fall a hundred times in the day, he would not despair. He would rather cry out lovingly to God, appealing to His tender pity. The really devout man has a horror of evil, but he has a still greater love of that which is good. He is more set on doing what is right than avoiding what is wrong. Generous and largehearted, he is not afraid of danger in serving God and would rather run the risk of doing His will imperfectly than not strive to serve Him lest he fail in the attempt.

Jean Nicolas Grou

*We have waited for him, and he will save us: this is the
LORD; we have waited for him, we will be glad...in his
salvation.* —Isaiah 25:9

> Blest are the humble souls that wait
> With sweet submission to His will;
> Harmonious all their passions move,
> And in the midst of storms are still.
>
> Philip Doddridge

*D*o not be discouraged at your faults. Bear with
yourself in correcting them, as you would with
your neighbor. Lay aside this ardor of mind, which
exhausts your body and leads you to commit errors.
Accustom yourself gradually to carry prayer into all
your daily occupations. Speak, move, and work in
peace, as if you were in prayer, as indeed you ought
to be. Do everything without excitement, by the
spirit of grace. As soon as you perceive your natural
impetuosity gliding in, retire quietly within, where
the kingdom of God is. Listen to the leadings of
grace. Then say and do nothing but what the Holy
Spirit will put in your heart. You will find that you
will become more tranquil, that your words will be
fewer and more effectual, and that, with less effort,
you will accomplish more good.

Fénelon

I have finished the work which thou gavest me to do.
—John 17:4

She hath done what she could. —Mark 14:8

He who God's will has borne and done,
    And his own restless longings stilled;
What else he does, or has foregone,
    His mission he has well fulfilled.
From a German Manuscript

Cheered by the presence of God, I will do at each moment, without anxiety, according to the strength that He will give me, the work that His providence assigns me. I will leave the rest without concern. It is not my affair. I ought to consider the duty to which I am called each day as the work that God has given me to do, and to apply myself to it in a manner worthy of His glory, that is to say, with exactness and in peace. I must neglect nothing. I must not be violent about anything.

Fénelon

It is your duty oftentimes to do what you do not want to do. It is your duty, too, to leave undone what you want to do.

Thomas à Kempis

Blessed be the Lord, who daily loadeth us with benefits.
—Psalm 68:19

Nor trust in uncertain riches, but in the living God,
who giveth us richly all things to enjoy.
—1 Timothy 6:17

Source of my life's refreshing springs,
    Whose presence in my heart sustains me,
Thy love ordains me pleasant things,
    Thy mercy orders all that pains me.

Anna Laetitia Waring

*A*nd to be true and speak my soul, when I survey the occurrences of my life and call into account the finger of God, I can perceive nothing but an immeasurable mass of mercies, either in general to mankind or in particular to myself. And I do not know whether this perception comes out of the prejudice of my affection, or an inverting and partial understanding of His mercies. But, those things that others term crosses, afflictions, judgments, misfortunes, both appear and, in event, have always proved to me, who inquires farther into them than their visible effects, to be the secret and disguised favors of His affection.

Sir Thomas Browne

February 13

The will of the Lord be done. —Acts 21:14

Let him do to me as seemeth good unto him.
—2 Samuel 15:26

To have, each day, the thing I wish,
  Lord, that seems best to me;
But not to have the thing I wish,
  Lord, that seems best to Thee.
Most truly, then, Thy will is done,
  When mine, O Lord, is crossed;
'T is good to see my plans o'erthrown,
  My ways in Thine all lost.

Horatius Bonar

O Lord, You know what is best for us. Let this or that be done, as You will please. Give what You will and how much You will and when You will. Deal with me as You think good. Set me where You will, and deal with me in all things just as You will. Behold, I am Your servant, prepared for all things, for I desire not to live unto myself, but unto You. Oh, that I could do it worthily and perfectly!

Thomas à Kempis

Dare to look up to God, and say, "Make use of me for the future as You will. I am of the same mind. I am one with You. I refuse nothing that seems good to You. Lead me where You will; clothe me in whatever dress You will. Is it Your will that I should be in a public or a private condition, dwell here or be banished, be poor or rich? Under all these circumstances, I will testify unto You before men."

Epictetus

February 14

But I would have you without carefulness.
—1 Corinthians 7:32

O Lord, how happy should we be
If we could cast our care on Thee,
 If we from self could rest;
And feel at heart that One above,
In perfect wisdom, perfect love,
 Is working for the best.

Joseph Anstice

*C*ast all your cares on God. See that all your cares be such as you can cast on God and then hold none back. Never brood over yourself. Never stop short in yourself, but cast your whole self, even this very thing that distresses you, upon God. Do not be anxious about little things, if you would learn to trust God with your all. Act upon faith in little things. Commit your daily cares and anxieties to Him, and He will strengthen your faith for any greater trials. Give your whole self into God's hands, and so trust Him to take care of you in all lesser things. Do this for His own sake, since You are His.

Edward B. Pusey

February 15

If ye fulfil the royal law according to the scripture,
Thou shalt love thy neighbour as thyself, ye do well.
—James 2:8

> Come, children, let us go!
> We travel hand in hand;
> Each in his brother finds his joy
> In this wild stranger land.
> The strong be quick to raise
> The weaker when they fall;
> Let love and peace and patience bloom
> In ready help for all.

Gerhard Tersteegen

*I*t is a sad weakness in us, after all, that the thought of a man's death consecrates him anew to us. It is as if life were not sacred too, as if it were comparatively a small thing to fail in love and reverence to the brother who has to climb the whole toilsome mountain with us. It seems as if all our tears and tenderness were due to the one who is spared that hard journey.

George Eliot

If we were to classify the laws that should reign in households, and whose daily transgression annoys and mortifies us and degrades our household life, we would learn to adorn every day with sacrifices. Good manners are made up of petty sacrifices. Temperance, courage, and love are made up of the same jewels. Listen to every prompting of honor.

Ralph Waldo Emerson

February 16

Serve him with a perfect heart and with a willing mind.
—1 Chronicles 28:9

And if some things I do not ask,
In my cup of blessing be,
I would have my spirit filled the more
With grateful love to Thee,
More careful,—not to serve Thee much,
But to please Thee perfectly.

Anna Laetitia Waring

Little things come daily, hourly, and within our reach, and they are not less calculated to set forward our growth in holiness than are the greater occasions that rarely occur. Moreover, fidelity in trifles, and an earnest seeking to please God in little matters, is a test of real devotion and love. Let your aim be to please our dear Lord perfectly in little things, and to attain a spirit of childlike simplicity and dependence. In proportion as self-love and self-confidence are weakened and our will is bowed to that of God, so will hindrances disappear. The internal troubles and contests that harassed the soul will vanish, and it will be filled with peace and tranquillity.

Jean Nicolas Grou

*My brethren, count it all joy when ye fall into divers
temptations [or trials]; knowing this, that the trying of
your faith worketh patience.* —James 1:2–3

For patience, when the rough winds blow!
    For patience, when our hopes are fading,
When visible things all backward go,
    And nowhere seems the power of aiding!
God still enfolds thee with His viewless hand,
And leads thee surely to the Fatherland.
    N. L. Frothingham, from a German Manuscript

*W*e have need of patience with ourselves and
with others, with those below and those
above us, and with our own equals. We need to be
patient with those who love us and those who do not
love us. Patience is also needed for the greatest
things and for the least, against sudden inroads of
trouble and under our daily burdens, with disappointments as to the weather or the breaking of the
heart. We have need of patience in the weariness of
the body or the wearing of the soul; in our own failure of duty or others' failure towards us; in everyday wants or in the aching of sickness or the decay
of age; in disappointment, bereavement, losses, injuries, reproaches; in heaviness of the heart or its
sickness amid delayed hopes. In all these things,
from childhood's little troubles to the martyr's sufferings, patience is the grace of God, whereby we
endure evil for the love of God.

Edward B. Pusey

It is good for me that I have been afflicted; that I might learn thy statutes. —Psalm 119:71

But though he cause grief, yet will he have compassion according to the multitude of his mercies.
—Lamentations 3:32

And yet these days of dreariness are sent us from above;
They do not come in anger, but in faithfulness and love;
They come to teach us lessons which bright ones could
not yield,
And to leave us blest and thankful when their purpose
is fulfilled.

Anonymous

*D*o not heed distressing thoughts when they rise ever so strongly in you. No, though they have entered you, do not fear them. Rather, be still awhile, not believing in the power that you feel they have over you, and they will suddenly fall. It is good for your spirit and greatly to your advantage to be much and variously tried by the Lord. You do not know what the Lord has already done and what He is yet doing for you in your spirit.

Isaac Penington

Why should I flinch at the plow of my Lord that makes deep furrows on my soul? I know He is no idle farmer. He purposes a crop.

Samuel Rutherford

February 19

My meat is to do the will of him that sent me, and to finish his work. —John 4:34

I am glad to think
I am not bound to make the world go right;
But only to discover and to do,
With cheerful heart, the work that God appoints.
I will trust in Him,
That He can hold His own; and I will take
His will, above the work He sendeth me,
To be my chiefest good.

Jean Ingelow

*D*on't object that your duties are so insignificant. They are to be reckoned of infinite significance, and important to you alone. If it is but the more perfect regulation of your house, the sorting of your clothes and trinkets, the arranging of your papers, *"whatsoever thy hand findeth to do, do it with thy might"* (Eccl. 9:10) and all your worth and constancy. It is much more important to do so if your duties are of evidently a higher, wider scope. If you have brothers, sisters, a father, a mother, weigh earnestly what claim lies upon you, on behalf of each. Consider it as one thing needful to pay them more and more honestly and nobly what you owe. What does it matter how miserable one is, if one can do that? That is the sure and steady disconnection and extinction of whatever miseries one has in this world.

Thomas Carlyle

February 20

Let us not therefore judge one another any more: but judge this rather, that no man put a stumblingblock or an occasion to fall in his brother's way.
—Romans 14:13

Them that were entering in ye hindered. —Luke 11:52

My mind was ruffled with small cares today,
And I said pettish words, and did not keep
Long-suffering patience well, and now how deep
My trouble for this sin! in vain I weep
For foolish words I never can unsay.

Henry Septimus Sutton

A vexation arises, and our expressions of impatience hinder others from taking it patiently. Disappointment, ailment, or even weather depresses us, and our look or tone of depression hinders others from maintaining a cheerful and thankful spirit. We say an unkind thing, and another is hindered in learning the holy lesson of charity that thinks no evil. We say a provoking thing, and our sister or brother is hindered in that day's effort to be meek. How sadly, too, we may hinder without word or act! For wrong feeling is more infectious than wrong doing, especially the various phases of ill temper: gloominess, touchiness, discontent, irritability. Do we not know how catching these are?

Frances Ridley Havergal

*If ye then, being evil, know how to give good gifts unto
your children, how much more shall your Father which
is in heaven give good things to them that ask him?*
—Matthew 7:11

For His great love has compassed
Our nature, and our need
We know not; but he knoweth,
And He will bless indeed.
Therefore, O heavenly Father,
Give what is best to me;
And take the wants unanswered,
As offerings made to Thee.

Anonymous

*W*hatever we ask for that is not for our good, He
will keep back from us. And surely in this
there is not less love than in the granting of what we
ought to desire. Will not the same love that prompts
you to give a good thing, prompt you to keep back an
evil thing? If, in our blindness, not knowing what to
ask, we pray for things that would turn in our hands
to sorrow and death, will not our Father, out of His
very love, deny us? How awful would our lots be if
our wishes would immediately pass into realities, if
we were endowed with a power to bring about all that
we desire, if the inclinations of our wills were followed by the fulfillment of our hasty wishes, and if
sudden longings were always granted. One day we
will bless Him, not more for what He has granted
than for what He has denied.

Cardinal Henry Edward Manning

Be careful for nothing; but in every thing by prayer and supplication with thanksgiving let your requests be made known unto God. —Philippians 4:6

> We tell Thee of our care,
> Of the sore burden, pressing day by day,
> And in the light and pity of Thy face,
> The burden melts away.
>
> We breathe our secret wish,
> The importunate longing which no man may see;
> We ask it humbly, or, more restful still,
> We leave it all to Thee.
>
> Susan Coolidge

*T*hat prayer which does not succeed in moderating our wish, in changing the passionate desire into still submission, the anxious, tumultuous expectation into silent surrender, is no true prayer and proves that we do not have the spirit of true prayer. That life is most holy in which there is least of petition and desire and most of waiting upon God. In a holy life, petition most often passes into thanksgiving. Pray until prayer makes you forget your own wish, and leave it or merge it in God's will. The Divine Wisdom has given us prayer, not as a means whereby to obtain the good things of earth, but as a means whereby we learn to do without them. He has given us prayer, not as a means whereby we escape trials, but as a means whereby we become strong to meet them.

Frederick William Robertson

Let the LORD do that which is good in his sight.
—1 Chronicles 19:13

Let thy mercy, O LORD, be upon us, according as we hope in thee. —Psalm 33:22

I cannot feel
That all is well, when darkening clouds conceal
The shining sun;
But then, I know
He lives and loves; and say, since it is so,
Thy will be done.

S. G. Browning

*N*o felt trial or defect becomes divine until it is impossible to overcome. Surrender only becomes possible when resistance to it is exhausted and hope has fled. The difficulty of our task lies here: that we have to strive against the grievous things of life while hope remains, as if they were harmful, and then when the stroke has fallen, to accept them from the hand of God and not doubt that they are good. But to the loving, trusting heart, all things are possible. And even this instant change from overstrained will to sorrowful repose, from fullest resistance to complete surrender, is realized without convulsion.

James Martineau

These things I have spoken unto you, that in me ye might have peace. In the world ye shall have tribulation: but be of good cheer; I have overcome the world.
—John 16:33

O Thou, the primal fount of life and peace,
    Who shedd'st Thy breathing quiet all around,
In me command that pain and conflict cease,
    And turn to music every jarring sound.
                   John Sterling

*A*ccustom yourself to unreasonableness and injustice. Abide in peace in the presence of God, who sees all these trials more clearly than you do, and who permits them. Be content with doing with calmness the little that depends upon yourself, and let all else be to you as if it were not.
                        Fénelon

It is rare when injustice, or slights patiently borne, do not leave the heart at the close of the day filled with marvelous joy and peace.
            Gold Dust, Published 1880

But now thus saith the LORD that created thee, O Jacob, and he that formed thee, O Israel, Fear not: for I have redeemed thee, I have called thee by thy name; thou art mine. —Isaiah 43:1

Thou art as much His care as if beside
   Nor man nor angel lived in heaven or earth;
Thus sunbeams pour alike their glorious tide,
   To light up worlds, or wake an insect's mirth.
John Keble

God beholds you individually, whoever you are. He calls *"thee by thy name."* He sees you and understands you. He knows what is in you, all your own peculiar feelings and thoughts, your dispositions and likings, your strength and your weakness. He views you in your day of rejoicing and your day of sorrow. He sympathizes with your hopes and with your temptations. He interests Himself in all your anxieties and your remembrances, in all the risings and fallings of your spirit. He surrounds you and bears you in His arms. He takes you up and sets you down. You do not love yourself better than He loves you. You cannot shrink from pain more than He dislikes your bearing it; and if He puts it on you, it is as you will put it on yourself, if you are wise, for a greater good afterwards.

Cardinal John Henry Newman

February 26

*The LORD is nigh unto all them that call upon him, to
all that call upon him in truth.* —Psalm 145:18

*I sought the LORD, and he heard me, and delivered me
from all my fears.* —Psalm 34:4

Be Thou, O Rock of Ages, nigh!
　　So shall each murmuring thought be gone;
And grief and fear and care shall fly,
　　As clouds before the mid-day sun.

Charles Wesley

*T*ake courage, and turn your troubles, which are
without remedy, into material for spiritual
progress. Often turn to our Lord, who is watching
you, poor frail little being as you are, amid your labors and distractions. He sends you help and blesses
your affliction. This thought should enable you to
bear your troubles patiently and gently for love of
Him who only allows you to be tried for your own
good. Raise your heart continually to God. Seek His
aid, and let the cornerstone of your consolation be
your happiness in being His. All vexations and an-
noyances will be comparatively unimportant while
you know that you have such a friend, such a stay,
such a refuge. May God be ever in your heart.

Francis de Sales

Trust in the LORD, and do good; so shalt thou dwell in the land, and verily thou shalt be fed. —Psalm 37:3

> Build a little fence of trust
>   Around today;
> Fill the space with loving work,
>   And therein stay;
> Look not through the sheltering bars
>   Upon tomorrow,
> God will help thee bear what comes,
>   Of joy or sorrow.
>
> Mary Frances Butts

Let us bow our souls and say, *"Behold the handmaid of the Lord"* (Luke 1:38). Let us lift up our hearts and ask, *"Lord, what wilt thou have me to do?"* (Acts 9:6). Then light from the opened heaven will stream on our daily task, revealing the grains of gold where yesterday all seemed to be dust. A hand will sustain us and our daily burden, so that, smiling at yesterday's fears, we will say, "This is easy, this is light." Every *"lion in the way"* (Prov. 26:13), as we come up to it, will be seen chained, and leave open the gates of the palace beautiful. And to us, even to us, feeble and fluctuating as we are, ministries will be assigned, and through our hands blessings will be conveyed in which the spirits of just men made perfect might delight.

Elizabeth Charles

Beloved, let us love one another: for love is of God; and every one that loveth is born of God, and knoweth God.
—1 John 4:7

> So to the calmly gathered thought
> The innermost of life is taught,
> The mystery, dimly understood,
> That love of God is love of good;
> That to be saved is only this,
> Salvation from our selfishness.
>
> John Greenleaf Whittier

*T*he spirit of Love, wherever it is, is its own blessing and happiness, because it is the truth and reality of God in the soul. Therefore, it has the same joy of life and is the same good to itself everywhere and on every occasion. Would you know the blessing of all blessings? It is this God of Love dwelling in your soul and killing every root of bitterness, which is the pain and torment of every earthly, selfish love. For all needs are satisfied; all disorders of nature are removed. Life is no longer a burden. Every day is a day of peace. Everything you meet becomes a help to you, because everything you see or do is all done in the sweet, gentle element of love.

William Law

Unto you that fear my name shall the Sun of righteousness arise with healing in his wings. —Malachi 4:2

O send out thy light and thy truth: let them lead me.
—Psalm 43:3

Open our eyes, thou Sun of life and gladness,
    That we may see that glorious world of Thine!
It shines for us in vain, while drooping sadness
    Enfolds us here like mist; come, Power benign,
      Touch our chilled hearts with vernal smile,
      Our wintry course do Thou beguile.
Nor by the wayside ruins let us mourn,
Who have th' eternal towers for our appointed bourn.
John Keble

*A*ll those scattered rays of beauty and loveliness, which we behold spread up and down over all the world, are only the emanations of that inexhausted Light which is above. We should therefore love them all and climb up always by those sunbeams unto the eternal Father of lights. We should look upon Him and take from Him the pattern of our lives. Always eyeing Him, we should, as Hierocles said, "polish and shape our souls into the clearest resemblance of Him." And, in all our behavior in this world (that great temple of His), we should behave decently and reverently with that humility, meekness, and modesty that suits His house.
Dr. John Smith

Take no thought for your life, what ye shall eat, or what ye shall drink; nor yet for your body, what ye shall put on. —Matthew 6:25

One there lives whose guardian eye
Guides our earthly destiny;
One there lives, who, Lord of all,
Keeps His children lest they fall;
Pass we then in love and praise,
Trusting Him through all our days,
Free from doubt and faithless sorrow,
God provideth for the morrow.

Reginald Heber

*I*t has been well said that no man ever sank under the burden of the day. It is when tomorrow's burden is added to the burden of today that the weight is more than a man can bear. Never load yourselves so, my friends. If you find yourselves so loaded, at least remember this: it is your own doing, not God's. He begs you to leave the future to Him, and mind the present.

George MacDonald

But to do good and to communicate forget not: for with such sacrifices God is well pleased. —Hebrews 13:16

For this is the message that ye heard from the beginning, that we should love one another. —1 John 3:11

Be useful where thou livest, that they may
Both want and wish thy pleasing presence still.
   ...Find our men's wants and will,
And meet them there. All worldly joys go less
To the one joy of doing kindnesses.

George Herbert

Let the weakest and the humblest remember that in his daily course he can, if he will, shed around him almost a heaven. Kind words, sympathizing attentions, watchfulness against wounding men's sensitiveness, these cost very little, but they are priceless in their value. Are they not almost the staple of our daily happiness? From hour to hour, from moment to moment, we are supported and blessed by small kindnesses.

Frederick William Robertson

Small kindnesses, small courtesies, small considerations, habitually practiced in our social interactions, give a greater charm to the character than the display of great talents and accomplishments.

Mary Anne Kelty

March 3

*I made haste, and delayed not to keep thy
commandments.* —Psalm 119:60

Ye know not what shall be on the morrow.
—James 4:14

Never delay
To do the duty which the hour brings,
Whether it be in great or smaller things;
For who doth know
What he shall do the coming day?

Anonymous

*I*t is quite impossible that an idle, floating spirit
can ever look up with clear eyes to God. It
spreads its miserable anarchy before the symmetry
of the creative Mind. In the midst of a disorderly
being that has neither center nor circumference, it
kneels beneath the glorious sky that everywhere has
both. And for a life that is all failure, it turns to the
Lord of the silent stars, the Lord whose conscientious thought of it is that *"not one faileth"* (Isa.
40:26). The heavens, with their everlasting faithfulness, look down on no sadder contradiction than the
sluggard and the slovenly in their prayers.

James Martineau

March 4

For all this I considered in my heart even to declare all this, that the righteous, and the wise, and their works, are in the hand of God. —Ecclesiastes 9:1

But souls that of His own good life partake,
He loves as His own self; dear as His eye
They are to Him: He'll never them forsake:
When they shall die, then God Himself shall die;
They live, they live in blest eternity.

Henry More

A good man might be very logically cunning, but he will not be so clever that he will be able to demonstrate his own immortality. Nevertheless, he sees it in a higher light. His soul, being purged and enlightened by true sanctity, is more capable of those divine irradiations whereby it feels itself in conjunction with God. It knows that God will never forsake His own life that He has quickened in it. He will never deny those ardent desires of a blissful fruition of Himself, which the lively sense of His own goodness has excited within it. Those breathings and gaspings after an eternal participation of Him are but the energy of His own breath within us. If He had had any mind to destroy it, He would never have shown it such things as He has done.

Dr. John Smith

March 5

And every man that hath this hope in him purifieth
himself, even as he is pure. —1 John 3:3

Now, Lord, what wait I for?
   On Thee alone
My hope is all rested,
   Lord, seal me Thine own!
Only Thine own to be,
Only to live to Thee.
      Thine, with each day begun,
      Thine, with each set of sun,
      Thine, till my work is done.

                                    Anna B. Warner

*N*ow, believe me, God hides some ideal in every human soul. At some time in our life we feel a trembling, fearful longing to do some good thing. Life finds its noblest spring of excellence in this hidden impulse to do our best. There is a time when we are not content to be such merchants or doctors or lawyers as we see uniformly every day. The woman longs to glorify her womanhood as sister, wife, or mother.

Here is God, God standing silently at the door all day long, God whispering to the soul that to be pure and true is to succeed in life, and whatever we get short of that will burn up like stubble, though the whole world try to save it.

                                    Robert Collyer

March 6

The shadow of a great rock in a weary land.
—Isaiah 32:2

In returning and rest shall ye be saved; in quietness and in confidence shall be your strength. —Isaiah 30:15

O Shadow in a sultry land!
  We gather to Thy breast,
Whose love, enfolding like the night,
  Brings quietude and rest,
Glimpse of the fairer life to be,
  In foretaste here possessed.

Caroline M. Packard

Strive to see God in all things without exception, and acquiesce in His will with absolute submission. Do everything for God, uniting yourself to Him by a mere upward glance or by the overflowing of your heart towards Him. Never be in a hurry. Do everything quietly and in a calm spirit. Do not lose your inward peace for anything whatsoever, even if your whole world seems upset. Commend all to God, and then lie still and be at rest in His bosom. Whatever happens, abide steadfast in a determination to cling simply to God, trusting in His eternal love for you. And if you find that you have wandered forth from this shelter, recall your heart quietly and simply. Maintain a holy simplicity of mind, and do not smother yourself with a host of cares, wishes, or longings, under any pretext.

Francis de Sales

There are diversities of operations, but it is the same God which worketh all in all. —1 Corinthians 12:6

I form the light, and create darkness: I make peace, and create evil: I the LORD do all these things.
—Isaiah 45:7

"All is of God that is, and is to be;
And God is good." Let this suffice us still,
Resting in childlike trust upon His will,
Who moves to His great ends, unthwarted by the ill.
John Greenleaf Whittier

*W*e can take it on faith, that everything is over-ruled to each of us by the all-holy and all-loving will of God. This includes the very least, or what seems to us great, every change of the seasons, everything that touches us in mind, body, or estate, whether brought about through this outward senseless nature or by the will of man, good or bad. Whatever befalls us, however it befalls us, we must receive as the will of God. If it befalls us through man's negligence or ill-will or anger, still it is, in even the least circumstance, to us the will of God. For if the least thing could happen to us without God's permission, it would be something out of God's control. God's providence or His love would not be what they are. Almighty God Himself would not be the same God, not the God whom we believe, adore, and love.

Edward B. Pusey

Study to show thyself approved unto God, a workman that needeth not to be ashamed. —2 Timothy 2:15

And let us not be weary in well doing: for in due season we shall reap, if we faint not. —Galatians 6:9

The task Thy wisdom hath assigned,
Oh, let me cheerfully fulfill;
In all my works Thy presence find,
And prove Thine acceptable will.

Charles Wesley

What is my next duty? What is the thing that lies nearest to me?" "That belongs to your everyday history. No one can answer that question but yourself. Your next duty is just to determine what your next duty is. Is there nothing you neglect? You would know your duty if you thought in earnest about it and were not ambitious of great things." "Ah, then," responded she, "I suppose it is something very commonplace, which will make life more dreary than ever. That cannot help me." "It will, if it is as dreary as reading the newspapers to an old deaf aunt. It will soon lead you to something more. Your duty will begin to comfort you at once, but will at length open the unknown fountain of life in your heart."

George MacDonald

Thou shalt rejoice before the LORD thy God in all that thou puttest thine hands unto. —Deuteronomy 12:18

Be ye thankful. —Colossians 3:15

Thou that hast given so much to me,
Give one thing more, a grateful heart.
Not thankful when it pleaseth me,
As if thy blessings had spare days;
But such a heart, whose pulse may be
     Thy praise.

George Herbert

*I*f anyone would tell you the shortest, surest way to all happiness and all perfection, he must tell you to make it a rule to yourself to thank and praise God for everything that happens to you. For it is certain that whatever seeming calamity happens to you, if you thank and praise God for it, you turn it into a blessing. Therefore, if you could work miracles, you could not do more for yourself than by this thankful spirit, for it heals with a word and turns all that it touches into happiness.

William Law

March 10

*When thou passest through the waters, I will be with
thee; and through the rivers, they shall not overflow
thee: when thou walkest through the fire, thou shalt not
be burned; neither shall the flame kindle upon thee.*
—Isaiah 43:2

I am with thee to deliver thee. —Jeremiah 1:8

When through the deep waters I call thee to go,
The rivers of sorrow shall not overflow;
For I will be with thee thy troubles to bless,
And sanctify to thee thy deepest distress.

Anonymous

*L*ook at it as you will, you must give yourself up
to suffer what is appointed you. If we did that,
God would bear us up at all times in all our sorrows
and troubles, and God would lay His shoulder under
our burdens and help us to bear them. For if, with a
cheerful courage, we submitted ourselves to God, no
suffering would be unbearable.

John Tauler

Learn to be as the angel who could descend
among the miseries of Bethesda without losing his
heavenly purity or his perfect happiness. Gain
healing from troubled waters. Make up your mind to
the prospect of sustaining a certain measure of pain
and trouble in your passage through life. By the
blessing of God this will prepare you for it. It will
make you thoughtful and resigned without inter-
fering with your cheerfulness.

Cardinal John Henry Newman

Cast thy burden upon the LORD, and he shall sustain thee: he shall never suffer the righteous to be moved.
—Psalm 55:22

Now our wants and burdens leaving,
To His care, who cares for all,
Cease we fearing, cease we grieving,
At His touch our burdens fall.
Samuel Longfellow

*T*he circumstances of her life she could not alter, but she took them to the Lord and handed them over into His management. Then she believed that He took it, and she left all the responsibility and the worry and anxiety with Him. As often as the anxieties returned she took them back to the Lord, and the result was that, although the circumstances remained unchanged, her soul was kept in perfect peace in the midst of them. And the secret she found so effectual in her outward affairs, she found to be still more effectual in her inward ones, which were in truth even more utterly unmanageable. She abandoned her whole self to the Lord with all that she was and all that she had. Believing that He took that which she had committed to Him, she ceased to fret and worry, and her life became all sunshine in the gladness of belonging to Him.

Hannah Whitall Smith

*The LORD bless thee, and keep thee: the LORD make his
face shine upon thee, and be gracious unto thee: the
LORD lift up his countenance upon thee, and give thee
peace.* —Numbers 6:24–26

> O Love, how cheering is Thy ray!
>> All pain before Thy presence flies;
> Care, anguish, sorrow, melt away,
>> Where'er Thy healing beams arise.
> O Father, nothing may I see,
> Nothing desire, or seek, but Thee.
>
> Paul Gerhardt

*T*here is a faith in God, and a clear perception of
His will and designs and providence and glory,
which gives to its possessor a confidence and patience and sweet composure. This faith can come
under every varied and troubling aspect of events,
such as no man can realize who has not felt its influences in his own heart. There is a communion
with God in which the soul feels the presence of the
unseen One in the profound depths of its being with
a vivid distinctness and a holy reverence such as no
words can describe. There is a state of union with
God—I do not say often reached, yet it has been attained in this world—in which all the past and present and future seem reconciled, and eternity won
and enjoyed. And then God and man, earth and
heaven, with all their mysteries, are seen in truth as
they lie in the mind of the Infinite.

Samuel Dowse Robbins

He that abideth in me, and I in him, the same bringeth forth much fruit. —John 15:5

Let the beauty of the LORD our God be upon us.
—Psalm 90:17

As some rare perfume in a vase of clay
    Pervades it with a fragrance not its own,
So, when Thou dwellest in a mortal soul,
    All heaven's own sweetness seems around it
        thrown.

Harriet Beecher Stowe

Some glances of real beauty may be seen in the faces of those who dwell in true meekness. There is a harmony in the sound of that voice to which divine love gives utterance. There is some appearance of right order in the temper and conduct of those whose passions are regulated.

John Woolman

I believe that no divine truth can truly dwell in any heart without an external testimony in manner, bearing, and appearance. This testimony will be a witness within the heart of the beholder, and will bear an unmistakable, though silent, evidence to the eternal principle from which it emanates.

Mary Anne Schimmelpenninck

March 14

I have called upon thee, for thou wilt hear me, O God:
incline thine ear unto me, and hear my speech.
—Psalm 17:6

Ye people, pour out your heart before him: God is a
refuge for us. —Psalm 62:8

Whate'er the care which breaks thy rest,
Whate'er the wish that swells thy breast;
Spread before God that wish, that care,
And change anxiety to prayer.

Anonymous

Whatever it is that burdens you, go tell your Father. Put the matter into His hand, and so you will be freed from that dividing, perplexing care that the world is full of. When you are either to do or suffer anything, when you are about any purpose or business, go tell God of it and acquaint Him with it. Yes, burden Him with it, and you are done with the matter of caring. There will be no more care, but quiet, sweet diligence in your duty and dependence on Him for the carriage of your matters. Roll your cares, and yourself with them, as one burden, all on your God.

Robert Leighton

Trouble and perplexity drive us to prayer, and prayer drives away trouble and perplexity.

Philip Melanchthon

Hear me, O LORD; for thy lovingkindness is good: turn unto me according to the multitude of thy tender mercies. —Psalm 69:16

Let, I pray thee, thy merciful kindness be for my comfort, according to thy word unto thy servant. —Psalm 119:76

> Love divine has seen and counted
> Every tear it caused to fall;
> And the storm which Love appointed
> Was its choicest gift of all.
>
> Anonymous*

Oh, that you could dwell in the knowledge and sense of this: that the Lord beholds your sufferings with pity and is able not only to uphold you under them, but also to do you good by them. Therefore, do not grieve at your lot. Do not be discontented. Do not look out at the hardness of your condition. But, when the storm and matters of vexation are sharp, look up to Him who can give meekness and patience, who can lift up your head over all, and who can cause your life to grow and achieve through all. If the Lord God helps you proportionately to your condition of affliction and distress, you will have no cause to complain, but to bless His name.

Isaac Penington

Whether therefore ye eat, or drink, or whatsoever ye do, do all to the glory of God. —1 Corinthians 10:31

With good will doing service, as to the Lord, and not to men. —Ephesians 6:7

> A servant, with this clause,
> Makes drudgery divine:
> Who sweeps a room, as for Thy laws,
> Makes that and th' action fine.
>
> George Herbert

Surely the truth must be that whatever in our daily lives is lawful and right for us to be engaged in, is in itself a part of our obedience to God, a part, that is, of our very religion. Whenever we hear people complaining of obstructions and hindrances put by the duties of life in the way of devoting themselves to God, we may be sure they are under some false view or another. They do not look upon their daily work as the task to which God has set them, and as obedience due to Him. We may go farther and say, not only are the duties of life, be they ever so toilsome and distracting, no obstructions to a life of any degree of inward holiness, but also that they are even direct means, when rightly used, to promote our sanctification.

Cardinal Henry Edward Manning

March 17

Where hast thou gleaned to day? —Ruth 2:19

What have I learnt where'er I've been,
From all I've heard, from all I've seen?
What know I more that's worth the knowing?
What have I done that's worth the doing?
What have I sought that I should shun?
What duties have I left undone?

                                        Pythagoras

All of this world will soon have passed away, but God will remain and you, whatever you have become, good or bad. Your deeds now are the seed of eternity. Each single act, in each particular day, good or bad, is a portion of that seed. Each day adds some line, making you more or less like Him, more or less capable of His love.

                                        Edward B. Pusey

There is something very solemn in the thought that the part of our work that we have left undone may first be revealed to us at the end of a life filled up, as we had fondly hoped, with useful and necessary employments.

                      Anna, or *Passages from Home Life*

Finally, be ye all of one mind, having compassion one of another, love as brethren, be pitiful, be courteous.
—1 Peter 3:8

> Make us of one heart and mind;
> Courteous, pitiful, and kind;
> Lowly, meek, in thought and word,
> Altogether like our Lord.
>
> Charles Wesley

A little thought will show you how vastly your own happiness depends on the way other people bear themselves toward you. The looks and tones at your breakfast table, the conduct of your fellow workers or employers, the faithful or unreliable men you deal with, what people say to you on the street, the letters you get, the friends or foes you meet— these things make up very much of the pleasure or misery of your day. Turn the idea around, and remember that just the same are you adding to the pleasure or the misery of other people's days. And this is the half of the matter that you can control. Whether any particular day will bring to you more of happiness or of suffering is largely beyond your power to determine. Whether each day of your life will give happiness or suffering to others rests with yourself.

George Spring Merriam

March 19

Showing all good fidelity; that they may adorn the doctrine of God our Saviour in all things. —Titus 2:10

> If on our daily course our mind
> Be set to hallow all we find,
> New treasures still, of countless price,
> God will provide for sacrifice.
>
> John Keble

*I*f contentment and thankfulness, or the patient bearing of evil, are duties to God, they are the duties of every day and in every circumstance of our lives. If we are to follow Christ, it must be in our common ways of spending every day.

William Law

He who is faithful over a few things is a lord of cities. It does not matter whether you preach in Westminster Abbey or teach a ragged class, as long as you are faithful. The faithfulness is all.

George MacDonald

I would have you invoke God often through the day. You should be asking Him to kindle a love for your vocation within you, and saying with Paul, "*'Lord, what wilt thou have me to do?'* (Acts 9:6). Would You have me serve You in the lowest ministries of Your house? I would be too happy to serve You in any way." And when any special thing goes against you, ask, "Would You have me do it? Then unworthy though I am, I will do it gladly."

Francis de Sales

Thou shalt worship the Lord thy God, and him only shalt thou serve. —Matthew 4:10

Blessed are they that keep his testimonies, and that seek him with the whole heart. —Psalm 119:2

> The comfort of a mind at rest
> From every care Thou hast not blest;
> A heart from all the world set free,
> To worship and to wait on Thee.
>
> Anna Laetitia Waring

*R*esign every forbidden joy. Restrain every wish that is not referred to His will. Banish all eager desires, all anxiety. Desire only the will of God. Seek Him alone, and you will find peace.

Fénelon

I've been a great deal happier since I have given up thinking about what is easy and pleasant, and being discontented because I couldn't have my own will. Our lives are determined for us, and it makes the mind very free when we give up wishing and only think of bearing what is laid upon us and doing what is given us to do.

George Eliot

Your heavenly Father knoweth that ye have need of all these things. —Matthew 6:32

All as God wills, who wisely heeds
　　To give or to withhold;
And knoweth more of all my needs
　　Than all my prayers have told.
　　　　　　　　　　John Greenleaf Whittier

*L*ord, I do not know what I ought to ask of You. You only know what we need. You love me better than I know how to love myself. O Father, give to Your child that for which he himself does not know how to ask. I dare not ask either for crosses or consolations. I simply present myself before You. I open my heart to You. Behold my needs that I do not know myself. See, and do according to Your tender mercy. Smite or heal. Depress me or raise me up. I adore all Your purposes without knowing them. I am silent. I offer myself in sacrifice. I yield myself to You. I would have no other desire than to accomplish Your will. Teach me to pray. Pray Yourself in me.

　　　　　　　　　　　　　　　Fénelon

Know ye not that a little leaven leaveneth the whole lump? Purge out therefore the old leaven, that ye may be a new lump, as ye are unleavened. —1 Corinthians 5:6–7

> One finger's-breadth at hand will mar
> A world of light in heaven afar,
> A mote eclipse a glorious star,
>   An eyelid hide the sky.

John Keble

A single sin, however apparently trifling or hidden in some obscure corner of our consciousness, which we do not intend to renounce, is enough to render real prayer impossible. A course of action not wholly upright and honorable, feelings not entirely kind and loving, habits not spotlessly chaste and temperate—any of these are impassable obstacles. If we know of a kind act that we might, but do not intend to, perform, if we are aware that our moral health requires the abandonment of some pleasure that yet we do not intend to abandon, here is cause enough for the loss of all spiritual power.

Frances Power Cobbe

It is astonishing how soon the whole conscience begins to unravel if a single stitch drops. One little sin indulged in makes a hole you could put your head through.

Charles Buxton

March 23

Beloved, thou doest faithfully whatsoever thou doest.
—3 John 1:5

And this also we wish, even your perfection.
—2 Corinthians 13:9

In all the little things of life,
Thyself, Lord, may I see;
In little and in great alike
Reveal Thy love to me.

So shall my undivided life
To Thee, my God, be given;
And all this earthly course below
Be one dear path to heaven.

Horatius Bonar

In order to mold you into entire conformity to His will, He must have you pliable in His hands. This pliability is more quickly reached by yielding in the little things than in the greater. Your one great desire is to follow Him fully. Can you not say then a continual "yes" to all His sweet commands, whether small or great, and trust Him to lead you by the shortest road to your fullest blessedness?

Hannah Whitall Smith

With meekness, humility, and diligence, apply yourself to the duties of your condition. They are the seemingly little things which make no noise that do the business.

Henry More

*I will both lay me down in peace, and sleep: for thou,
LORD, only makest me dwell in safety.* —Psalm 4:8

He giveth his beloved sleep. —Psalm 127:2

He guides our feet, He guards our way,
His morning smiles bless all the day;
He spreads the evening veil, and keeps
The silent hours while Israel sleeps.

Isaac Watts

*W*e sleep in peace in the arms of God when we
yield ourselves up to His providence in a delightful consciousness of His tender mercies. There
are no more restless uncertainties, no more anxious
desires, and no more impatience at the places we are
in, for it is God who has put us there and who holds
us in His arms. Can we be unsafe where He has
placed us?

Fénelon

One evening when Luther saw a little bird
perched on a tree, to roost there for the night, he
said, "This little bird has had its supper. Now it is
getting ready to go to sleep here, quite secure and
content, never troubling itself what its food will be,
or where its lodging on the morrow. Like David, it
'abide[s] *under the shadow of the Almighty'* (Ps.
91:1). It sits on its little twig, content, and lets God
take care."

Anonymous

I will hear what God the LORD will speak: for he will speak peace unto his people. —Psalm 85:8

There is a voice, "a still, small voice" of love
> Heard from above;
But not amidst the din of earthly sounds,
> Which here confounds;
By those withdrawn apart it best is heard,
And peace, sweet peace, breathes in each gentle word.

Anonymous

He speaks, but it is with us to listen or not. It is much, yes, it is everything, not to turn away the ear, to be willing to listen, not to drown His voice. *"The secret of the LORD is with them that fear him"* (Ps. 25:14). It is a secret, hushed voice, a gentle intercourse of heart to heart, a still, small voice, whispering to the inner ear. How will we hear it if we fill our ears and our hearts with the din of this world? How will we hear it if we fill ourselves with the world's empty tumult, its excitement, its fretting vanities or cares or passions or anxieties or show or rivalries, and its whirl of emptinesses?

Edward B. Pusey

Are they not all ministering spirits? —Hebrews 1:14

> May I reach
> That purest heaven, be to other souls
> The cup of strength in some great agony,
> Enkindle generous ardor, feed pure love,
> Be the sweet presence of a good diffused,
> And in diffusion ever more intense!
> So shall I join the choir invisible
> Whose music is the gladness of the world.
>
> George Eliot

Certainly, in our own little sphere, it is not the most active people to whom we owe the most. Among the common people whom we know, it is not necessarily those who are busiest, not those who, meteor-like, are always on the rush after some visible charge and work. We look up to and gather the deepest calm and courage from the lives that, like the stars, simply pour down on us the calm light of their bright and faithful beings. It seems to me that there is reassurance here for many of us who seem to have no chance for active usefulness. We can do nothing for our fellowmen. But still it is good to know that we can be something for them. It is good to know, and this we may know surely, that no man or woman of the humblest sort can really be strong, gentle, pure, and good, without the world being better for it, without somebody being helped and comforted by the very existence of that goodness.

Phillips Brooks

*If we love one another, God dwelleth in us, and his love
is perfected in us.* —1 John 4:12

*And he that keepeth his commandments dwelleth in
him, and he in him. And hereby we know that he abideth in us, by the Spirit which he hath given us.*
—1 John 3:24

Abide in me; o'ershadow by Thy love
Each half-formed purpose and dark thought of sin,
Quench, ere it rise, each selfish, low desire,
And keep my soul as Thine, calm and divine.

Harriet Beecher Stowe

*T*he spirit of love must work the works and
speak the tones of love. It cannot exist and give
no sign or a false sign. It cannot be a spirit of love
and disguise itself with irritable and selfish impatience. It cannot be a spirit of love and at the same
time make self the prominent object. It cannot rejoice to lend itself to the happiness of others and at
the same time be seeking its own. It cannot be generous and envious. It cannot be sympathizing and
improper, self-forgetful and boastful. It cannot delight in the rectitude and purity of other hearts, as
the spiritual elements of their peace, and yet unnec-
essarily suspect them.

John Hamilton Thom

Giving thanks always for all things unto God.
—Ephesians 5:20

For blessings of the fruitful season,
　　For work and rest, for friends and home,
For the great gifts of thought and reason.
　　To praise and bless Thee, Lord, we come.

Yes, and for weeping and for wailing,
　　For bitter hail and blighting frost,
For high hopes on the low earth trailing,
　　For sweet joys missed, for pure aims crossed.
　　　　　　　　　　　　　　Eliza Scudder

*N*otwithstanding all that I have suffered, all the pain and weariness and anxiety and sorrow that necessarily enter into life, and the inward errings that are worse than all, I would end my record with devout thanksgiving to the great Author of my being. For more and more am I unwilling to make my gratitude to Him what is commonly called "a thanksgiving for mercies" for any benefits or blessings that are peculiar to myself, my friends, or indeed to any man. Instead of this, I would be grateful for all that belongs to my life and being: for joy and sorrow, for health and sickness, for success and disappointment, for virtue and for temptation, for life and death. I would have to do this because I believe that all is meant for good.

Orville Dewey

March 29

There shall no evil befall thee. —Psalm 91:10

*Whoso hearkeneth unto me shall dwell safely, and shall
be quiet from fear of evil.* —Proverbs 1:33

I ask not, "Take away this weight of care";
No, for that love I pray that all can bear,
    And for the faith that whatsoe'er befall
Must needs be good, and for my profit prove,
Since from my Father's heart most rich in love,
    And from His bounteous hands it cometh all.
                    Carl Johann Philipp Spitta

*B*e like the promontory against which the waves continually break. It stands firm and tames the fury of the water around it. Am I unhappy because this has happened to me? Not so, but I am happy, though this has happened to me, because I continue to be free from pain, neither crushed by the present nor fearing the future. Will then this which has happened prevent you from being just, magnanimous, temperate, prudent, and secure against inconsiderate opinions and falsehood? Remember, too, on every occasion that leads you to vexation to apply this principle: that this is not a misfortune, but that to bear it nobly is good fortune.

                    Marcus Aurelius Antoninus

Thou shalt guide me with thy counsel, and afterward receive me to glory. —Psalm 73:24

There remaineth therefore a rest to the people of God. —Hebrews 4:9

> Guide us through life; and when at last
> We enter into rest,
> Thy tender arms around us cast,
> And fold us to Thy breast.
>
> Henry Francis Lyte

*G*o forth to meet the solemnities and to conquer the trials of existence, believing in a Shepherd of your souls. Then faith in Him will support you in duty, and duty firmly done will strengthen faith. At last, then, when all is over here, your faith will raise the song of conquest. The noise and strife of the earthly battle will have faded upon your dying ear, and you will hear, instead, the deep and musical sound of the ocean of eternity and see the lights of heaven shining on its waters still and fair in their radiant rest. In its retrospect of the life that has ended, and in its forward glance upon the life to come, take up the poetic inspiration of the Hebrew king: *"Surely goodness and mercy shall follow me all the days of my life: and I will dwell in the house of the LORD for ever"* (Ps. 23:6).

Stopford A. Brooke

March 31

Thou shalt be in league with the stones of the field: and
the beasts of the field shall be at peace with thee. And
thou shalt know that thy tabernacle shall be in peace.
—Job 5:23–24

Love had he found in huts where poor men lie;
His daily teachers had been woods and rills,
The silence that is in the starry sky,
The sleep that is among the lonely hills.
William Wordsworth

*T*he spirit that suffices quiet hearts, comes forth
to the poor and hungry and to those who are of
simple taste. This spirit seems to come forth to such
from every dry knoll of withered grass, from every
pine stump and half-embedded stone on which the
dull March sun shines. If you fill your brain with
Boston and New York, with fashion and covetous-
ness, and will stimulate your jaded senses with wine
and French coffee, you will find no radiance of wisdom in the lonely waste of the pine-woods.
Ralph Waldo Emerson

April 1

For God so loved the world. —John 3:16

We love him, because he first loved us. —1 John 4:19

> He prayeth best who loveth best
>   All things both great and small;
> For the dear God who loveth us,
>   He made and loveth all.
>
> Samuel Taylor Coleridge

*T*o know that love alone was the beginning of nature and creature is a reflection that must be quite ravishing to every intelligent creature that is sensible of it. It is to know that nothing but love encompasses the whole universe of things. It is to know that the governing Hand that overrules all, the watchful Eye that sees through all, is nothing but omnipotent and omniscient Love, using an infinity of wisdom to save every misguided creature from the miserable works of its own hands, and make happiness and glory the perpetual inheritance of all the creation.

William Law

April 2

Know ye not that ye are the temple of God, and that the Spirit of God dwelleth in you? —1 Corinthians 3:16

> Father! replenish with Thy grace
> This longing heart of mine;
> Make it Thy quiet dwelling place
> Thy sacred inmost shrine!
>
> Angelus Silesius

Man's manifold cares, not his manifold labors, hinder the presence of God. Whatever you do, hush yourself to your own feverish vanities and busy thoughts and cares. In silence seek your Father's face, and the light of His countenance will stream down upon you. He will make a secret place in your heart, and when you enter there, there you will find Him. And if you have found Him there, all around will reflect Him, all will speak to Him, and He will speak through all. Outwardly you may be doing the work of your calling. Inwardly, if you commend your work to God, you may be with Him in the third heaven.

Edward B. Pusey

April 3

As for thee, the LORD thy God hath not suffered thee so to do. —Deuteronomy 18:14

> Lord, for the erring thought
> Not into evil wrought;
> Lord, for the wicked will
> Betrayed and baffled still;
> For the heart from itself kept,
> Our Thanksgiving accept.
>
> William Dean Howells

*W*hat an amazing and blessed disproportion between the evil we do and the evil we are capable of doing, and seem sometimes on the very verge of doing! If my soul has grown tares, when it was full of the seeds of nightshade, how happy ought I to be! And that the tares have not wholly strangled the wheat, what a wonder it is! We ought to thank God daily for the sins we have not committed.

Frederick William Faber

We give thanks often with a tearful, doubtful voice, for our spiritual mercies *positive,* but what an almost infinite field there is for mercies negative! We cannot even imagine all that God has allowed us *not* to do, *not* to be.

Frances Ridley Havergal

You are surprised at your imperfections—why? I should infer from that, that your self-knowledge is small. Surely, you might rather be astonished that you do not fall into more frequent and more grievous faults, and thank God for His upholding grace.

Jean Nicolas Grou

April 4

Well done, good and faithful servant; thou hast been faithful over a few things, I will make thee ruler over many things: enter thou into the joy of thy lord.
—Matthew 25:23

O Father! help us to resign
  Our hearts, our strength, our wills to Thee;
Then even lowliest work of Thine
  Most noble, blest, and sweet will be.
Harriet McEwen Kimball

*N*othing is too little to be ordered by our Father. Nothing is too little in which to see His hand. Nothing is too little that touches our souls, too little to accept from Him. Nothing is too little to be done for Him.

Edward B. Pusey

A soul occupied with great ideas best performs small duties. The most divine views of life penetrate most clearly into the basest emergencies. Far from petty principles being best proportioned to petty trials, a heavenly spirit taking up its abode with us can alone sustain well the daily toils. This spirit can tranquilly endure the humiliations of our condition.

James Martineau

Whoever neglects a thing that he suspects he ought to do, because it seems to him too small a thing, is deceiving himself. It is not too little, but too great for him that he does not do it.

Edward B. Pusey

April 5

*Yet I have left me seven thousand in Israel, all the knees
which have not bowed unto Baal, and every mouth
which hath not kissed him.* —1 Kings 19:18

Back then, complainer; loathe thy life no more,
Nor deem thyself upon a desert shore,
    Because the rocks the nearer prospect close.
Yet in fallen Israel are there hearts and eyes
That day by day in prayer like thine arise:
    Thou know'st them not, but their Creator knows.

John Keble

A man went down to the great school with a another lesson in his heart: the lesson that he who
has conquered his own coward spirit has conquered
the whole world. In addition, he learned the same
lesson that the prophet learned in the cave in Mount
Horeb, when he hid his face, and the still small voice
asked, *"What doest thou here, Elijah?"* (1 Kings
19:13). He learned that however we may fancy ourselves alone on the side of good, the King and Lord of
men is nowhere without His witnesses, for in every
society, however seemingly corrupt and godless, there
are those who have not bowed their knees to Baal.

Thomas Hughes

So then, Elijah's life had not been a failure after
all. Seven thousand at least in Israel had been braced
and encouraged by his example and silently blessed
him, perhaps, for the courage that they felt. In God's
world there is no failure for those who are in earnest.
No work truly done, no word earnestly spoken, no
sacrifice freely made, was ever made in vain.

Frederick William Robertson

April 6

*In the multitude of my thoughts within me thy comforts
delight my soul.* —Psalm 94:19

*Perplexed, but not in despair…cast down, but not
destroyed.* —2 Corinthians 4:8–9

> Discouraged in the work of life,
>   Disheartened by its load,
> Shamed by its failures or its fears,
>   I sink beside the road;
> But let me only think of Thee,
> And then new heart springs up in me.
>
>   Samuel Longfellow

*D*iscouragement is an inclination to give up all attempts after the devout life, in consequence of the difficulties by which it is beset, and because of our already numerous failures in it. We lose heart, and partly in ill-temper, partly in real doubt of our own ability to persevere, we first grow irritable and cross with God. Then we relax in our efforts to mortify ourselves and to please Him. It is a sort of shadow of despair and will lead us into numberless venial sins the first half-hour we give way to it.

                                   Frederick William Faber

Never let us be discouraged with ourselves. It is not when we are conscious of our faults that we are the most wicked. On the contrary, we are less so. We see by a brighter light. Let us remember for our consolation that we never perceive our sins until we begin to cure them.

                                   Fénelon

That ye may prove what is that good, and acceptable, and perfect, will of God. —Romans 12:2

Thou knowest what is best;
    And who but Thee, O God, hath power to know?
In Thy great will my trusting heart shall rest;
    Beneath that will my humble head shall bow.

                Thomas Cogswell Upham

*T*o those who are His, all things are not only easy to be borne, but even to be gladly chosen. Their wills are united to the will that moves heaven and earth, that gives laws to angels and rules the courses of the world. It is a wonderful gift of God to man, for man to be at the center of that motion where everlasting rest is and to be sheltered in the peace of God. It is a gift to dwell even now in heaven where all hearts are stayed and all hopes fulfilled. *"Thou wilt keep him in perfect peace, whose mind is stayed on thee"* (Isa. 26:3).

             Cardinal Henry Edward Manning

Study to follow His will in all, to have no will but His. This is your duty and your wisdom. Nothing is gained by spurning and struggling except to hurt and vex yourself, but by complying sweet peace is gained. It is the very secret, the mystery of solid peace within, to resign all to His will, to be disposed of at His pleasure, without the least contrary thought.

                Robert Leighton

April 8

The LORD is my shepherd; I shall not want.
            —Psalm 23:1

They that seek the LORD shall not want any good thing.
            —Psalm 34:10

> God, who the universe doth hold
>   In his fold,
> Is my shepherd kind and heedful,
> Is my shepherd, and doth keep
>   Me, his sheep,
> Still supplied with all things needful.
>
>   Francis Davison

*W*ho is it that is your shepherd? The Lord! Oh, my friends, what a wonderful announcement! The Lord God of heaven and earth, the almighty Creator of all things, He who holds the universe in His hand as though it were a very little thing, He is your shepherd and has charged Himself with the care and keeping of you, as a shepherd is charged with the care and keeping of his sheep. If your hearts could really take in this thought, you would never have a fear or a care again. For with such a shepherd, how could it be possible for you ever to lack any good thing?

                    Hannah Whitall Smith

April 9

Watch and pray, that ye enter not into temptation.
    —Matthew 26:41

I want a sober mind,
    A self-renouncing will,
That tramples down and casts behind
    The baits of pleasing ill;
A spirit still prepared,
    And armed with jealous care,
Forever standing on its guard,
    And watching unto prayer.

Charles Wesley

*W*hen you say, *"Lead us not into temptation"* (Matt. 6:13), you must earnestly intend to avoid in your daily conduct those temptations which you have already suffered from. When you say, *"Deliver us from evil"* (Matt. 6:13), you must intend to struggle against that evil in your hearts, which you are conscious of, and for which you pray to be forgiven. To watch and pray are surely in our power, and by these means we are certain of getting strength. Do you feel your weakness? Do you fear to be overcome by temptation? Then keep out of the way of it. This is watching. Avoid society that is likely to mislead you. Flee from the very shadow of evil. You cannot be too careful. Better be a little too strict than a little too easy; it is the safer side. Abstain from reading books that are dangerous to you. Turn from bad thoughts when they arise.

Cardinal John Henry Newman

April 10

And whatsoever ye do, do it heartily, as to the Lord, and not unto men. —Colossians 3:23

Not with eyeservice, as menpleasers; but in singleness of heart, fearing God. —Colossians 3:22

> Teach me, my God and King,
> In all things Thee to see,
> And what I do in anything,
> To do it as for Thee.
>
> George Herbert

*T*here is no action so slight or so common but it may be done to a great purpose and therefore be ennobled. Nor is any purpose so great but that slight actions may help it, and may be so done as to help it much. Most especially, these actions will help that chief of all purposes: the pleasing of God.

John Ruskin

Every duty, even the least duty, involves the whole principle of obedience. And little duties make the will dutiful, that is, supple and prompt to obey. Little obediences lead into great ones. The daily round of duty is full of examination and discipline. It trains the will, heart, and conscience. We need not be prophets or apostles. The commonest life may be full of perfection. The duties of home are a discipline for the ministries of heaven.

Cardinal Henry Edward Manning

April 11

Wherefore, beloved...be diligent that ye may be found of him in peace, without spot, and blameless.
—2 Peter 3:14

His conscience knows no secret stings,
    While grace and joy combine
To form a life whose holy springs
    Are hidden and divine.

Isaac Watts

Even the smallest discontent of conscience may render the whole temper of the mind turbid. But, only produce the effort that restores its peace, and over the whole atmosphere a breath of unexpected purity is spread. Doubt and irritation pass away as clouds. The withered sympathies of earth and home open their leaves and live. And through the clearest blue the deep is seen of the heaven where God resides.

James Martineau

The state of mind that is described as meekness, or quietness of spirit, is characterized in a high degree by inward harmony. There is not, as formerly, that inward jarring of thought contending with thought, and conscience asserting rights that it could not maintain.

Thomas Cogswell Upham

April 12

Be perfect, be of good comfort, be of one mind, live in peace; and the God of love and peace shall be with you.
—2 Corinthians 13:11

He that loveth not his brother whom he hath seen, how can he love God whom he hath not seen? —1 John 4:20

> Lord! Subdue our selfish will;
>   Each to each our tempers suit,
> By Thy modulating skill,
>   Heart to heart, as lute to lute.
>
> Charles Wesley

*I*t requires far more of the constraining love of Christ to love our cousins and neighbors as members of the heavenly family than to feel the heart warm to our suffering brothers and sisters in Tuscany or Madeira. To love the whole church is one thing. To love, that is, to delight in the graces and veil the defects, of the person who misunderstood me and opposed my plans yesterday, whose peculiar infirmities grate on my most sensitive feelings, or whose natural faults are precisely those from which my natural character most revolts, is quite another.

Elizabeth Charles

April 13

*In all these things we are more than conquerors
through him that loved us.* —Romans 8:37

Thus my soul before her God
    Lieth still, nor speaketh more,
Conqueror thus o'er pain and wrong,
    That once smote her to the core;
Like a silent ocean, bright
With her God's great praise and light.

                Johann Joseph Winkler

*M*y mind is forever closed against embarrassment and perplexity, against uncertainty, doubt, and anxiety. My heart is closed against grief and desire. Calm and unmoved, I look down on all things, for I know that I cannot explain a single event, nor comprehend its connection with that which alone concerns me. In His world all things prosper. This satisfies me, and in this belief I stand fast as a rock. My breast is steeled against annoyance on account of personal offenses and vexations, or exultation in personal merit, for my whole personality has disappeared in the contemplation of the purpose of my being.

                Johann Gottlieb Fichte

April 14

For all things are yours; whether Paul, or Apollos, or Cephas, or the world, or life, or death, or things present, or things to come; all are yours; and ye are Christ's; and Christ is God's. —1 Corinthians 3:21–23

As having nothing, and yet possessing all things.
—2 Corinthians 6:10

> Old friends, old scenes, will lovelier be,
> As more of Heaven in each we see:
> Some softening gleam of love and prayer
> Shall dawn on every cross and care.
>   John Keble

*O*ut of love and hatred; out of earnings and borrowings and lendings and losses; out of sickness and pain; out of wooing and worshipping; out of traveling and voting and watching and caring; out of disgrace and contempt; comes our instruction in the serene and beautiful laws. Let him not slur his lesson. Let him learn it by heart. Let him endeavor exactly, bravely, and cheerfully to solve the problem of that life which is set before him. And this problem will be solved by punctual action, not by promises or dreams. Believing, as in God, in the presence and favor of the grandest influences, let him deserve that favor and learn how to receive and use it, by fidelity also to the lower observances.

                                     Ralph Waldo Emerson

We know that all things work together for good to them that love God. —Romans 8:28

As for you, ye thought evil against me; but God meant it unto good. —Genesis 50:20

> Ill that He blesses is our good,
> And unblest good is ill;
> And all is right that seems most wrong,
> If it be His sweet Will.
>
> Frederick William Faber

*T*o those who know themselves, all things work together for good, and all things seem to be, as they are to them, good. The goods that God gives seem *"very good"* (Gen. 1:31), and God Himself in them, because they know that they do not deserve them. The evils that God allows and overrules also seem *"very good,"* because they see in them His loving hand, put forth to heal them of what shuts out God from the soul. They love God intensely in that He is so good to them in each, in every, in the least good, because it is more than they deserve. How much more in the greatest! They love God for every and each, the very greatest of what seem evils, knowing them to be, from His love, real goods. For He by whom all the hairs of our head are numbered (Matt. 10:30), and who knows what we are made of, directs everything that befalls us in life, in perfect wisdom and love, to the well-being of our souls.

Edward B. Pusey

The very God of peace sanctify you wholly; and I pray God your whole spirit and soul and body be preserved blameless unto the coming of our Lord Jesus Christ. Faithful is he that calleth you, who also will do it.
—1 Thessalonians 5:23–24

Be still, my soul!—the Lord is on thy side;
    Bear patiently the cross of grief and pain;
Leave to thy God to order and provide,
    In every change He faithful will remain.
                    Hymns from the Land of Luther

It was no relief from temporal evils that the apostle promised. No, the mercy of God might send them to the stake or the lions. It was still His mercy if it but kept them *"unspotted from the world"* (James 1:27). It might expose them to insult, calumny, and wrong. They still received it as mercy if it established them *"in every good word and work"* (2 Thess. 2:17). O brothers and sisters! How many of you are content with such faithfulness as this on the part of your heavenly Father? Is this, indeed, the tone and tenor of your prayers?

                                    William Archer Butler

April 17

Blessed is that man that maketh the LORD his trust.
—Psalm 40:4

That we may lead a quiet and peaceable life.
—1 Timothy 2:2

> Just to let thy Father do
> What He will;
> Just to know that He is true,
> And be still;
> Just to trust Him, this is all!
> Then the day will surely be
> Peaceful, whatsoe'er befall,
> Bright and blessèd, calm and free.
>
> Frances Ridley Havergal

*E*very morning compose your soul for a tranquil day, and all through it be careful often to recall your resolution and bring yourself back to it, so to speak. If something discomposes you, do not be upset or troubled; but having discovered the fact, humble yourself gently before God, and try to bring your mind into a quiet attitude. Say to yourself, "Well, I have made a false step. Now I must go more carefully and watchfully." Do this each time, however frequently you fall. When you are at peace, use it profitably, making constant acts of meekness and seeking to be calm even in the most trifling things. Above all, do not be discouraged. Be patient; wait. Strive to attain a calm, gentle spirit.

Francis de Sales

*What doth the LORD thy God require of thee, but to fear
the LORD thy God, to walk in all his ways, and to love
him, and to serve the LORD thy God with all thy heart
and with all thy soul?* —Deuteronomy 10:12

What asks our Father of His children save
　　Justice and mercy and humility,
　　A reasonable service of good deeds,
　　Pure living, tenderness to human needs,
Reverence, and trust, and prayer for light to see
　　The Master's footprints in our daily ways?
　　　　No knotted scourge, nor sacrificial knife,
　　　　But the calm beauty of an ordered life
Whose every breathing is unworded praise.
　　　　　　　　　　　John Greenleaf Whittier

*G*ive yourself up to God without reserve, in singleness of heart. Meet everything that every day
brings forth as something that comes from God and
is to be received and gone through by you in such a
heavenly use of it, as you would suppose the holy
Jesus would have done in such occurrences. This is
an attainable degree of perfection.

　　　　　　　　　　　　　William Law

We ought to measure our actual lot and to fulfill it, to be with all our strength that which our lot
requires and allows. What is beyond it is no calling
of ours. How much peace, quiet, confidence, and
strength would people attain if they would go by
this plain rule.

　　　　　　　　Cardinal Henry Edward Manning

April 19

The hand of our God is upon all them for good that seek him. —Ezra 8:22

Into thine hand I commit my spirit. —Psalm 31:5

Thou layest Thy hand on the fluttering heart,
    And sayest, "Be still!"
The silence and shadow are only a part
    Of Thy sweet will;
Thy presence is with me, and where Thou art
    I fear no ill.

Frances Ridley Havergal

*B*e still and cool in your own mind and spirit from your own thoughts. Then you will feel the principle of God to turn your mind to the Lord God, from whom life comes, whereby you may receive His strength and power to allay all blustering storms and tempests. That is what works itself up into patience, into innocence, into soberness, into stillness, into steadiness, into quietness, up to God with His power. Therefore, be still awhile from your own thoughts, searching, seeking, desires, and imaginations. And, be confident of the principle of God in you, that it may raise your mind up to God and keep it upon Him. You will then find strength from Him and find Him to be a God at hand, a present help in the time of trouble and need.

George Fox

April 20

I waited patiently for the LORD; and he inclined unto me, and heard my cry. —Psalm 40:1

Tribulation worketh patience; and patience, experience; and experience, hope. —Romans 5:3–4

Lord, we have wandered forth through doubt and sorrow
   And Thou hast made each step an onward one;
And we will ever trust each unknown morrow,
   Thou wilt sustain us till its work is done.
Samuel Johnson

*I*t is possible—when the future is dim, when our depressed faculties can form no bright ideas of the perfection and happiness of a better world—it is possible still to cling to the conviction of God's merciful purpose towards His creatures, of His parental goodness even in suffering. We can still feel that the path of duty, though trodden with a heavy heart, leads to peace. We can still be true to conscience. We can still do our work, resist temptation, be useful, though with diminished energy, and give up our wills, even when we cannot rejoice under God's mysterious providence. In this patient, though uncheered, obedience, we become prepared for light. The soul gathers force.

William Ellery Channing

April 21

*Whom having not seen, ye love; in whom, though now
ye see him not, yet believing, ye rejoice with joy unspeakable and full of glory.* —1 Peter 1:8

If ye love me, keep my commandments. —John 14:15

> Blest be Thy love, dear Lord,
> That taught us this sweet way,
> Only to love Thee for Thyself,
> And for that love obey.
>
> John Austin

*T*o love God is to love His character. For instance, God is purity. And to be pure in
thought and look, to turn away from unhallowed
books and conversation, to abhor the moments in
which we have not been pure, is to love God. God is
love, and to love men until private attachments
have expanded into a philanthropy that embraces
all—at last even the evil and enemies with compassion—that is to love God. God is truth. To be true,
to hate every form of falsehood, to live a brave, true,
real life, is to love God. God is infinite. So, to love
the boundless, reaching on from grace to grace,
adding charity to faith, and rising upwards ever to
see the ideal still above us, and to die with it unat-
tained, aiming insatiably to be perfect even as the
Father is perfect—that is to love God.

Frederick William Robertson

Enter thou into the joy of thy lord. —Matthew 25:23

Serving the Lord; rejoicing in hope.
—Romans 12:11–12

If our love were but more simple,
We should take Him at His word;
And our lives would be all sunshine
In the sweetness of our Lord.
Frederick William Faber

*W*hat would it be to love absolutely a being absolutely lovely? What would it be to be able to give our whole existence, every thought, every act, every desire, to that adored One? What would it be to know that He accepts it all and loves us in return as God alone can love? This happiness grows forever. The larger our natures become, the wider our scope of thought, the stronger our will, the more fervent our affections, the deeper must be the rapture of such God-granted prayer. Every sacrifice *resolved on* opens wide the gate. Every sacrifice *accomplished* is a step towards the paradise within. Soon it will be no transitory glimpse, no rapture of a day, to be followed by clouds and coldness. Let us but labor and pray and wait. Then the intervals of human frailty will grow shorter and less dark, the days of our delight in God longer and brighter, until at last life will be nothing but His love. Our eyes will never grow dim. His smile will never turn away.

Frances Power Cobbe

April 23

These were the potters, and those that dwelt among plants and hedges: there they dwelt with the king for his work. —1 Chronicles 4:23

> A lowlier task on them is laid,
>   With love to make the labor light;
> And there their beauty they must shed
>   On quiet homes, and lost to sight.
> Changed are their visions high and fair,
> Yet, calm and still, they labor there.
>
> *Hymns of the Ages*

Anywhere and everywhere we may dwell *"with the king for his work."* We may be in a very unlikely or unfavorable place for this. It may be in a literal country life, with little enough to be seen of the *"goings"* of the King around us (Ps. 68:24). It may be among hedges of all sorts, hindrances in all directions. It may be, furthermore, with our hands full of all manner of pottery for our daily task. No matter! The King who placed us there will come and dwell there with us. The hedges are all right, or He would soon do away with them. And it does not follow that what seems to hinder our way may not be for its very protection. And as for the pottery, why, that is just exactly what He has seen fit to put into our hands, and therefore it is, for the present, *"his work."*

Frances Ridley Havergal

Bear ye one another's burdens, and so fulfil the law of Christ. —Galatians 6:2

> Is thy cruse of comfort wasting?
> Rise and share it with another,
> And through all the years of famine,
> It shall serve thee and thy brother.
> Is thy burden hard and heavy?
> Do thy steps drag heavily?
> Help to bear thy brother's burden;
> God will bear both it and thee.
>
> Elizabeth Charles

*H*owever perplexed you may at any hour become about some question of truth, one refuge and resource is always at hand: you can do something for someone besides yourself. When your own burden is heaviest, you can always lighten a little some other burden. At the times when you cannot see God, there is still open to you this sacred possibility: to *show* God. For it is the love and kindness of human hearts through which the divine reality comes home to men, whether they name it or not. Let this thought, then, stay with you: there may be times when you cannot find help, but there is no time when you cannot give help.

George Spring Merriam

April 25

Surely I have behaved and quieted myself, as a child that is weaned of his mother: my soul is even as a weaned child. —Psalm 131:2

Quiet, Lord, my froward heart,
Make me teachable and mild,
Upright, simple, free from art,
Make me as a weaned child;
From distrust and envy free,
Pleased with all that pleaseth Thee.

John Newton

Oh, do not look after great things. Small breathings, small desires after the Lord, if true and pure, are sweet beginnings of life. Take heed of despising *"the day of small things"* (Zech. 4:10) by looking after some great visitation, proportional to your distress, from your own viewpoint. No, you must become a child. You must lose your own will little by little. You must wait for life to be measured out by the Father, and be content with what proportion, and at what time, He will please to measure.

Isaac Penington

"When Israel was a child, then I loved him" (Hos. 11:1). Aim to be always this little child, contented with what the Father gives of pleasure or of play. And when restrained from pleasure or from play, and led for a season into the chamber of sorrow, rest quietly on His bosom and be patient and smile as one who is nestled in a sweet and secure shelter.

Anonymous

If we hope for that we see not, then do we with patience wait for it. —Romans 8:25

One day is with the Lord as a thousand years, and a thousand years as one day. —2 Peter 3:8

> Lord! who Thy thousand years dost wait
> To work the thousandth part
> Of Thy vast plan, for us create
> With zeal a patient heart.
> Cardinal John Henry Newman

Our heavenly Father intends us to have soul beauty and perfection and glory and a glorious and lovely spiritual body that this soul is to dwell in through all eternity. I believe that if we could only see this beforehand, if we could have a glimpse of this, we would not grudge all the trouble and pains He is taking with us now to bring us up to that ideal, which is His thought of us. We know that it is God's way to work slowly, so we must not be surprised if He takes a great many years of discipline to turn a mortal being into an immortal, glorious angel.

Annie Keary

April 27

Speak ye every man the truth to his neighbour.
    —Zechariah 8:16

*For our rejoicing is this, the testimony of our
conscience, that in simplicity and godly sincerity...
we have had our conversation in the world.*
    —2 Corinthians 1:12

Appear I always what I am?
    And am I what I am pretending?
    Know I what way my course is bending?
And sound my word and thought the same?
                                        Anonymous

Am I acting in simplicity from a germ of the divine life within, or am I shaping my path to obtain some immediate result of expediency? Am I endeavoring to obtain effects amidst a tangled web of foreign influences I cannot calculate? Or am I seeking simply to do what is right and leaving the consequences to the good providence of God?
                            Mary Anne Schimmelpenninck

Let it not be in any man's power to say truly of you that you are not simple or that you are not good, but let him be a liar whoever will think anything of this kind about you. This is altogether in your power. For who is he that will hinder you from being good and simple?
                            Marcus Aurelius Antoninus

April 28

The LORD is thy keeper: the LORD is thy shade upon thy right hand. —Psalm 121:5

Great peace have they which love thy law: and nothing shall offend them. —Psalm 119:165

> I rest beneath the Almighty's shade,
>   My griefs expire, my troubles cease;
> Thou, Lord, on whom my soul is stayed,
>   Wilt keep me still in perfect peace.
>
> Charles Wesley

One great sign of the practical recognition of the divine moment, and of our finding God's habitation in it, is constant calmness and peace of mind. Events and things come with the moment, but God comes with them too. If He comes in the sunshine, we find rest and joy. And if He comes in the storm, we know He is King of the storms, and our hearts are not troubled. God Himself, though possessing a heart filled with the tenderest feelings, is, nevertheless, an everlasting tranquillity. When we enter into His holy tabernacle, our souls necessarily enter into the tabernacle of rest.

Thomas Cogswell Upham

My soul was not only brought into harmony with itself and with God but with God's providences. In the exercise of faith and love, I endured and performed whatever came in God's providence, in submission, in thankfulness, and silence.

Madame Jeanne Guyon

I will arise and go to my father. —Luke 15:18

> O my God, my Father! hear,
>> And help me to believe;
> Weak and weary I draw near;
>> Thy child, O God, receive.
> I so oft have gone astray;
>> To the perfect Guide I flee;
> Thou wilt turn me not away,
>> Thy love is pledged to me.
>
> *Hymns of the Spirit*

O child, have you fallen? Arise, and go with childlike trust to your Father, like the prodigal son, and humbly say, with heart and mouth, *"Father, I have sinned against heaven, and before thee, and am no more worthy to be called thy son: make me as one of thy hired servants"* (Luke 15:18–19). And what will your heavenly Father do but what that father did in the parable? Assuredly, He will not change His essence, which is love, for the sake of your misdoings. Is it not His own precious treasure, and a small thing with Him, to forgive you your trespasses if you believe in Him? For His hand is not shortened that it cannot make you fit to be saved.

John Tauler

April 30

Speak unto the children of Israel, that they go forward.
—Exodus 14:15

No man, having put his hand to the plow, and looking
back, is fit for the kingdom of God. —Luke 9:62

Be trustful, be steadfast, whatever betide thee,
Only one thing do thou ask of the Lord,
Grace to go forward wherever He guide thee,
Simply believing the truth of His word.
                                                    Anonymous

*T*he soul ceases to weary itself with planning
and foreseeing by giving itself up to God's Holy
Spirit within, and to the teachings of His providence
without. He is not forever fretting as to his progress
or looking back to see how far he is getting on.
Rather, he goes steadily and quietly on and makes
all the more progress because it is unconscious. So
he never gets troubled and discouraged. If he falls,
he humbles himself but gets up at once and goes on
with renewed earnestness.

                                        Jean Nicolas Grou

May 1

*I will bless the LORD at all times: his praise shall con-
tinually be in my mouth.* —Psalm 34:1

*I will praise thee, O LORD, with my whole heart; I will
show forth all thy marvellous works.* —Psalm 9:1

> Thrice blest will all our blessings be,
> When we can look through them to Thee;
> When each glad heart its tribute pays
> Of love and gratitude and praise.
>
> M. J. Cotterill

*T*hat which befits us, embosomed in beauty and
wonder as we are, is cheerfulness and courage
and the endeavor to realize our aspirations. Will not
the heart, which has received so much, trust the
Power by which it lives? May it not quit other leadings and listen to the soul that has guided it so and
taught it so much, secure that the future will be
worthy of the past?

Ralph Waldo Emerson

I have experienced that the habit of taking out
of the hand of our Lord every little blessing and
brightness on our path, confirms us, in an especial
manner, in communion with His love.

Mary Anne Schimmelpenninck

The ornament of a meek and quiet spirit, which is in the sight of God of great price. —1 Peter 3:4

To present you holy and unblameable and unreproveable in his sight. —Colossians 1:22

> Thy sinless mind in us reveal,
> Thy spirit's plenitude impart!
> Till all my spotless life shall tell
> The abundance of a loving heart.
>
> Charles Wesley

*H*oliness appeared to me to be of a sweet, pleasant, charming, serene, calm nature. It seemed to me it brought an inexpressible purity, brightness, peacefulness, and ravishment to the soul. It seemed also that it made the soul like a field or garden of God, with all manner of pleasant flowers, that is all pleasant, delightful, and undisturbed, enjoying a sweet calm and the gentle life-giving beams of the sun. The soul of a true Christian appeared like a little white flower such as we see in the spring of the year. It was low and humble on the ground, opening its bosom to receive the pleasant beams of the sun's glory, rejoicing, as it were, in a calm rapture, diffusing around a sweet fragrance. It was standing peacefully and lovingly in the midst of other flowers round about, all in like manner opening their bosoms to drink in the light of the sun.

Jonathan Edwards

*The LORD is good, a strong hold in the day of trouble;
and he knoweth them that trust in him.* —Nahum 1:7

Leave God to order all thy ways,
    And hope in Him, whate'er betide
Thou 'lt find Him in the evil days
    Thy all-sufficient strength and guide;
Who trusts in God's unchanging love,
Builds on the rock that nought can move.

Georg Neumarck

Our whole trouble in our lots in this world rises from the disagreement of our minds with it. Let our minds concentrate on our places in the world, and the whole tumult is instantly hushed. Let it be kept in that disposition, and the man will stand at ease in his affliction, like a rock unmoved with waters beating upon it.

Thomas Boston

How does our will become sanctified? By conforming itself unreservedly to that of God. We will all that He wills and will nothing that He does not will. We attach our feeble will to that all-powerful will which performs everything. Thus nothing can ever come to pass against our will, for nothing can happen except that which God wills. And we find in His good pleasure an inexhaustible source of peace and consolation.

Fénelon

May 4

Who through faith subdued kingdoms, wrought right-eousness, obtained promises, stopped the mouths of lions...out of weakness were made strong.
—Hebrews 11:33–34

She met the hosts of Sorrow with a look
    That altered not beneath the frown they wore,
And soon the lowering brood were tamed, and took,
    Meekly, her gentle rule, and frowned no more.
Her soft hand put aside the assaults of wrath,
      And calmly broke in twain
      The fiery shafts of pain,
And rent the nets of passion from her path.
    By that victorious hand despair was slain;
With love she vanquished hate, and overcame
    Evil with good, in her great Master's name.
                William Cullen Bryant

*A*s to what may befall us outwardly in this confused state of things, will we not trust our tender Father and rest satisfied in His will? Will anything hurt us? Can tribulation, distress, persecution, famine, nakedness, peril, or sword come between the love of the Father to the child? Or can any of these things disturb the child's rest, contentment, or delight in His love? And does not the love, the rest, the peace, the joy felt, swallow up all the bitterness and sorrow of the outward condition?
                Isaac Penington

*If thou hast run with the footmen, and they have wea-
ried thee, then how canst thou contend with horses? and
if in the land of peace, wherein thou trustedst, they wearied thee, then how wilt thou do in the swelling of
Jordan?* —Jeremiah 12:5

> How couldst thou hang upon the cross,
> To whom a weary hour is loss?
> Or how the thorns and scourging brook,
> Who shrinkest from a scornful look?
>
> John Keble

A heart unloving among kindred has no love towards God's saints and angels. If we have a cold
heart towards a servant or a friend, why should we
wonder if we have no fervor towards God? If we are
cold in our private prayers, we would be earthly and
dull in the most devout religious order. If we cannot
bear the vexations of a companion, how will we bear
the contradiction of sinners? If a little pain over-
comes us, how could we endure a cross? If we have
no tender, cheerful, affectionate love to those with
whom our daily hours are spent, how can we feel the
pulse and ardor of love to the unknown and the evil,
the ungrateful and repulsive?

Cardinal Henry Edward Manning

May 6

Be kindly affectioned one to another with brotherly love.
—Romans 12:10

In her tongue is the law of kindness. —Proverbs 31:26

> Since trifles make the sum of human things,
> And half our misery from our foibles springs;
> Since life's best joys consist in peace and ease,
> And though but few can serve yet all can please;
> Oh, let the ungentle spirit learn from hence,
> A small unkindness is a great offence.
>
> Hannah More

*A*ll usefulness and all comfort may be prevented by an unkind, sour, irritable temper of mind—a mind that can bear with no difference of opinion or temperament. A spirit of faultfinding; an unsatisfied temper; a constant irritability; little inequalities in the look, the temper, or the manner; a brow cloudy and dissatisfied—your husband or your wife cannot tell why—will more than neutralize all the good you can do and render life anything but a blessing.

Albert Barnes

You have not fulfilled every duty, unless you have fulfilled that of being pleasant.

Charles Buxton

May 7

He healeth the broken in heart, and bindeth up their wounds. He telleth the number of the stars; he calleth them all by their names. —Psalm 147:3–4

Teach me your mood, O patient stars!
　　Who climb each night the ancient sky,
Leaving on space no shade, no scars,
　　No trace of age, no fear to die.
　　　　　　　　　　　　Ralph Waldo Emerson

I looked up to the heavens once more, and the quietness of the stars seemed to reproach me. "We are safe up here," they seemed to say. "We shine, fearless and confident, for the God who gave the primrose its rough leaves to hide it from the blast of uneven spring, hangs us in the awful hollows of space. We cannot fall out of His safety. Lift up your eyes on high and behold! Who has created these things? Who brings out their host by number? He calls them all by names. By the greatness of His might, for He is strong in power, not one fails. *'Why sayest thou, O Jacob, and speakest, O Israel, My way is hid from the LORD, and my judgment is passed over from my God?'* (Isa. 40:27)."

　　　　　　　　　　　　George MacDonald

May 8

This is the day which the LORD hath made; we will rejoice and be glad in it. —Psalm 118:24

Why stand ye here all the day idle? —Matthew 20:6

So here hath been dawning another blue day;
Think, wilt thou let it slip useless away?
Out of eternity this new day is born;
Into eternity at night will return.

Thomas Carlyle

*S*mall cares or deficiencies in the arrangement and ordering of our lives, daily trouble our hearts and cross the clearness of our faculties. These entanglements hang around us and leave us no free soul able to give itself up, in power and gladness, to the true work of life. The severest training and self-denial, which are superior to the servitude of indulgence, are the indispensable conditions even of pleasant spirits, of unclouded energies, of tempers free from morbidness. They are even more the conditions of the practiced and vigorous mind, ready at every call, and thoroughly furnished unto all good works.

John Hamilton Thom

True, we can never be at peace until we have performed the highest duty of all, until we have arisen and gone to our Father. But the performance of smaller duties, yes, even of the smallest, will do more to give us temporary repose, will act more as healthy pain-killers, than the greatest joys that can come to us from any other part of life.

George MacDonald

The LORD gave, and the LORD hath taken away; blessed be the name of the LORD. —Job 1:21

What Thou hast given, Thou canst take,
And when Thou wilt new gifts can make.
　All flows from Thee alone;
When Thou didst give it, it was Thine;
When Thou retook'st it, 't was not mine.
　Thy will in all be done.

John Austin

*W*e are ready to praise when all shines fair. But such is not the case when life is overcast; when all things seem to be against us; when we are in fear for some cherished happiness, or in the depths of sorrow, or in the solitude of a life that has no visible support, or in a season of sickness with the shadow of death approaching. To praise God then is a true sacrifice of praise. It is a sacrifice of praise to say, "This fear, loneliness, affliction, pain, and trembling awe are as sure tokens of love, as life, health, joy, and the gifts of home. *'The LORD gave, and the LORD hath taken away.'* On either side it is He, and all is love alike. *'Blessed be the name of the LORD.'*" What can come amiss to a soul that is so in accord with God? What can make so much as one jarring tone in all its harmony? In all the changes of this fitful life, it always dwells in praise.

Cardinal Henry Edward Manning

The LORD redeemeth the soul of his servants: and none
of them that trust in him shall be desolate.
—Psalm 34:22

Though he slay me, yet will I trust in him. —Job 13:15

I praise Thee while my days go on;
I love Thee while my days go on:
Through dark and dearth, through fire and frost,
With emptied arms and treasure lost,
I thank Thee while my days go on.

Elizabeth Barrett Browning

*T*he sickness of the last week was fine medicine.
Pain disintegrated the spirit, or became spiritual. I rose—I felt that I had given to God more perhaps than an angel could. I had promised Him in youth that to be a blot on this fair world, at His command, would be acceptable. I constantly offer myself to continue the obscurest and loneliest thing ever heard of, with one condition, His agency. Yes, I want to love You, and all You do, while You shed frost and darkness on every path of mine.

Mary Moody Emerson

Shall we receive good at the hand of God, and shall we not receive evil? —Job 2:10

Thou hast dealt well with thy servant, O LORD, according unto thy word. —Psalm 119:65

> Whatsoe'er our lot may be,
> Calmly in this thought we'll rest,
> Could we see as Thou dost see,
> We should choose it as the best.
>
> William Gaskell

*I*t is a proverbial saying, that everyone makes his own destiny. This is usually interpreted that everyone by his wise or unwise conduct prepares good or evil for himself. But we may also understand it that whatever it is that one receives from the hand of Providence, he may so accommodate himself to it that he will find his lot good for him, however much he may seem to others to be wanting.

Karl Wilhelm von Humboldt

Evil, once bravely confronted, ceases to be evil. There is generous battle hope in place of dead, passive misery. The evil itself has become a kind of good.

Thomas Carlyle

Fear none of those things which thou shalt suffer...ye shall have tribulation ten days: be thou faithful unto death, and I will give thee a crown of life.
—Revelation 2:10

Then, O my soul, be ne'er afraid,
On Him who thee and all things made
    Do thou all calmly rest;
Whate'er may come, where'er we go,
Our Father in the heavens must know
    In all things what is best.

Paul Flemming

Guide me, O Lord, in all the changes and varieties of the world. Guide me so that in all things that will happen, I may have an evenness and tranquility of spirit. Guide me so that my soul may be wholly resigned to Your most divine will and pleasure, never murmuring at Your gentle chastisements and fatherly correction. Amen.

Jeremy Taylor

You are never at any time nearer to God than when under tribulation, which He permits for the purification and beautifying of your soul.

Miguel Molinos

Prize inward exercises, griefs, and troubles, and let faith and patience have their perfect work in them.

Isaac Penington

I pray not that thou shouldest take them out of the world, but that thou shouldest keep them from the evil.
—John 17:15

In busy mart and crowded street,
No less than in the still retreat,
Thou, Lord, art near, our souls to bless,
With all a Father's tenderness.

Isaac Williams

Only the individual conscience, and He who is greater than the conscience, can tell where worldliness prevails. Each heart must answer for itself and at its own risk. That our souls are committed to our own keeping, at our own peril, in a world so mixed as this, is the last reason we should slumber over the charge or betray the trust. That outlet to the Infinite should be kept open, and the inner bond with eternal life preserved. Not one movement of this world's business is to be interfered with, nor one pulse-beat of its happiness repressed. All natural associations need to be dear and cherished, with all human sympathies fresh and warm. Then we will yet be near to the kingdom of heaven, within the order of the cosmos of God. We will be in the world, but not of the world—not taken out of it, but kept from its evil.

John Hamilton Thom

*And what doth the LORD require of thee, but to do
justly, and to love mercy, and to walk humbly with thy
God?* —Micah 6:8

*Put on therefore...kindness, humbleness of mind,
meekness, longsuffering.* —Colossians 3:12

> Plant in us an humble mind,
> Patient, pitiful, and kind;
> Meek and lowly let us be,
> Full of goodness, full of Thee.
>
> Charles Wesley

*T*here is no true and constant gentleness without humility. While we are so fond of ourselves, we are easily offended with others. Let us be persuaded that nothing is due to us, and then nothing will disturb us. Let us often think of our own infirmities, and we will become indulgent towards those of others.

Fénelon

Endeavor to be patient in bearing with the defects and infirmities of others, of what sort they may be, because you also have many failings that must be borne with by others. If you cannot make yourself such a one as you would, how can you expect to have another in all things to your liking?

Thomas à Kempis

May 15

My presence shall go with thee, and I will give thee rest.
—Exodus 33:14

Thou wilt show me the path of life: in thy presence is
fulness of joy; at thy right hand there are pleasures for
evermore. —Psalm 16:11

Thy presence fills my mind with peace,
    Brightens the thoughts so dark erewhile,
Bids cares and sad forebodings cease,
    Makes all things smile.

Charlotte Elliott

*H*ow will we rest in God? By giving ourselves
wholly to Him. If you give yourself by halves,
you cannot find full rest. There will always be a
lurking disquiet in the half that is withheld. Martyrs, confessors, and saints have tasted this rest,
and counted themselves happy in that they endured
(James 5:11). A countless host of God's faithful servants have drunk deeply of it under the daily burden of a weary life, dull, commonplace, painful, or
desolate. All that God has been to them, He is ready
to be to you. When the heart is once fairly given to
God, with a clear conscience, a fitting rule of life,
and a steadfast purpose of obedience, you will find a
wonderful sense of rest coming over you.

Jean Nicolas Grou

Finally, my brethren, be strong in the Lord, and in the power of his might. —Ephesians 6:10

No man can serve two masters. —Matthew 6:24

> Oh, there are heavenly heights to reach
>   In many a fearful place,
> Where the poor timid heir of God
>   Lies blindly on his face;
> Lies languishing for grace divine
>   That he shall never see
> Till he go forward at Thy sign,
>   And trust himself to Thee.
>
> Anna Laetitia Waring

*R*eservations, which concern some unhallowed sentiments or habits in the present, or some possibly impending temptations in the future, lie dormant in the mind. Thus do we cheat ourselves of inward and outward joys together. We give up many an indulgence for conscience' sake but stop short at that point of entire faithfulness wherein conscience could reward us. If we would but give ourselves wholly to God—give up, for the present and the future, every act, and, above all, every thought and every feeling, to be all purified to the uttermost, and rendered the best, noblest, holiest we can conceive—then would sacrifice bear with it a peace, rendering itself, I truly believe, far easier than before.

Frances Power Cobbe

May 17

Wherefore comfort yourselves together, and edify one another, even as also ye do. —1 Thessalonians 5:11

Thou shalt love thy neighbour as thyself.
—Matthew 19:19

So others shall
Take patience, labor, to their heart and hand,
From thy hand, and thy heart, and thy brave cheer,
And God's grace fructify through thee to all.
The least flower with a brimming cup may stand,
And share its dewdrop with another near.

Elizabeth Barrett Browning

What is meant by "our neighbor" we cannot doubt. It is everyone with whom we are brought into contact. First of all, he is literally our neighbor who is next to us in our own family and household: husband to wife, wife to husband, parent to child, brother to sister, master to servant, servant to master. Then it is he who is close to us in our own neighborhood, in our own town, in our own parish, on our own street. With these all true charity begins. To love and be kind to these is the very beginning of all true religion. But, besides these, as our Lord teaches, our neighbor is everyone who is thrown across our path by the changes and chances of life; he or she, whoever it is, whom we have any means of helping. It is the unfortunate stranger whom we may meet in traveling, the deserted friend whom no one else cares to look after.

Arthur Penrhyn Stanley

We know that we have passed from death unto life, because we love the brethren. —1 John 3:14

He that loveth not knoweth not God; for God is love.
—1 John 4:8

> Mutual love the token be,
> Lord, that we belong to Thee,
> Love, Thine image, love impart;
> Stamp it on our face and heart;
> Only love to us be given;
> Lord, we ask no other heaven.
>
> Charles Wesley

Oh, how many times most of us can remember when we would gladly have made any compromise with our consciences, would gladly have made the most costly sacrifices to God, if He would only have excused us from this duty of loving, of which our nature seemed utterly incapable. It is far easier to feel kindly, to act kindly, toward those with whom we are seldom brought into contact, whose tempers and prejudices do not rule against ours, and whose interests do not clash with ours, than to keep up a habitual, steady, self-sacrificing love towards those whose weaknesses and faults are always forcing themselves upon us and are stirring up our own. A man may be a good philanthropist despite being but a poor master to his servants, or father to his own children.

John Frederick Denison Maurice

Rest in the LORD, and wait patiently for him.
—Psalm 37:7

Trust in him at all times. —Psalm 62:8

Dost thou ask when comes His hour?
Then, when it shall aid thee best.
Trust His faithfulness and power,
Trust in Him, and quiet rest.

Anonymous

I had found communion with God to consist not only in the silencing of the outward man, but also in the silencing of every thought and in the concentration of the soul and all its powers into a simple, quiet watching and waiting for the food that its heavenly Father might see fit either to give or to withhold. In no case could it be sent away empty. For if comfort, light, or joy were withheld, the act of humble waiting at the gate of heavenly wisdom could not but work patience in it and thus render it, by humility and obedience, more *"meet to be* [a partaker] *of the inheritance of the saints in light"* (Col. 1:12), and also more blessed in itself.

Mary Anne Kelty

"Rest in the LORD, and wait patiently for him." In Hebrew, "Be silent to God, and let Him mold you." Keep still, and He will mold you to the right shape.

Martin Luther

To be spiritually minded is life and peace.
—Romans 8:6

Stilled now be every anxious care;
See God's great goodness everywhere;
Leave all to Him in perfect rest:
He will do all things for the best.

From a German Manuscript

*W*e should all endeavor and labor for a calmer spirit, so that we may the better serve God in praying to Him and praising Him. And, we should serve one another in love so that we may be fitted to do and receive good, that we may make our passage to heaven easier and more cheerful without allowing our wings to droop. So much as we are quiet and cheerful upon good ground, so much we live and are, as it were, in heaven.

Richard Sibbes

Keep yourself as much as you possibly can in peace, not by any effort, but by letting all things that trouble or excite you fall to the ground. This is not work, but it is, as it were, setting down a fluid to settle that has become turbid through agitation.

Madame Jeanne Guyon

The beloved of the LORD shall dwell in safety by him;
and the LORD shall cover him all the day long.
—Deuteronomy 33:12

Whate'er events betide,
  Thy will they all perform;
Safe in Thy breast my head I hide,
  Nor fear the coming storm.

Henry Francis Lyte

I have seemed to see a need of everything God gives me and need nothing that He denies me. There is no dispensation, though afflictive, but either in it, or after it, I find that I could not be without it. Whether it is taken from or not given to me, sooner or later God quiets me in Himself without it. I cast all my concerns on the Lord and live securely on the care and wisdom of my heavenly Father. My ways are, in a sense, hedged up with thorns and grow darker and darker daily. Yet I do not distrust my good God in the least and live more quietly in the absence of all by faith than I would do, I am persuaded, if I possessed them.

Anonymous

May 22

He that dwelleth in the secret place of the most High
shall abide under the shadow of the Almighty.
—Psalm 91:1

> They who on the Lord rely,
> Safely dwell though danger's nigh;
> Lo! His sheltering wings are spread
> O'er each faithful servant's head.
> When they wake, or when they sleep,
> Angel guards their vigils keep;
> Death and danger may be near,
> Faith and love have nought to fear.
>
> Harriet Auber

There shall no evil befall thee, neither shall any plague come nigh thy dwelling" (Ps. 91:10), is a promise to the fullest extent verified in the case of all who dwell *"in the secret place of the most High."* To them, sorrows are not evils, sicknesses are not plagues. The shadow of the Almighty extending far around those who abide under it alters the character of all things that come within its influence.

Anonymous

It is faith's work to claim and challenge loving-kindness out of all the roughest strokes of God.

Samuel Rutherford

May 23

Be content with such things as ye have. —Hebrews 13:5

I have learned, in whatsoever state I am, therewith to be content. —Philippians 4:11

> No longer forward nor behind
> I look in hope or fear;
> But, grateful, take the good I find,
> The best of now and here.
>
> John Greenleaf Whittier

If we wish to gain contentment, we might try such rules as these: (1) Allow yourself to complain of nothing, not even of the weather. (2) Never picture yourself to yourself under any circumstances in which you are not. (3) Never compare your own lot with that of another. (4) Never allow yourself to dwell on the wish that this or that had been, or were, otherwise than it was, or is. God Almighty loves you better and more wisely than you do yourself. (5) Never dwell on the morrow. Remember that it is God's, not yours. The heaviest part of sorrow often is to look forward to it. *"God will provide"* (Gen. 22:8).

Edward B. Pusey

*Now no chastening for the present seemeth to be joyous,
but grievous: nevertheless afterward it yieldeth the
peaceable fruit of righteousness unto them which are
exercised thereby.* —Hebrews 12:11

I cannot say,
Beneath the pressure of life's cares today,
I joy in these;
But I can say
That I had rather walk this rugged way,
If Him it please.

S. G. Browning

*W*hatever seems not joyous, but grievous, is
linked in *"the good pleasure of his goodness"*
(2 Thess. 1:11). It could be the particular annoyance
that befell you this morning, the vexatious words
that met your ear and grieved your spirit, the disappointment that was His appointment for today, or
the slight but hindering ailment. It could be as well
the presence of someone who is *"a grief of mind"*
(Gen. 26:35) to you. This *"good pleasure"* has a cor-
responding afterward of *"peaceable fruit,"* the very
seed from which, if you only do not choke it, will
spring and ripen.

Frances Ridley Havergal

O my Father, if it be possible, let this cup pass from me:
nevertheless not as I will, but as thou wilt.
—Matthew 26:39

O Lord my God, do Thou Thy holy will,
    I will lie still.
I will not stir, lest I forsake Thine arm,
    And break the charm
Which lulls me, clinging to my Father's breast,
    In perfect rest.

John Keble

*R*esignation to the will of God is the whole of piety. It includes in it all that is good and is a source of the most settled quiet and composure of mind. Our resignation to the will of God may be said to be perfect when our will is lost and resolved into His, when we rest in His will as our end, as being itself most just and right and good. And where is the impossibility of such an affection to what is just and right and good, such a loyalty of heart to the Governor of the universe, as will prevail over all sinister indirect desires of our own?

Bishop Joseph Butler

There are no disappointments to those whose wills are buried in the will of God.

Frederick William Faber

Lord, Your will be done in father, mother, child, in everything and everywhere, without a reserve, without a *but,* an *if,* or a limit.

Francis de Sales

May 26

The LORD heareth your murmurings which ye murmur against him. —Exodus 16:8

> Without murmur, uncomplaining,
> In His hand,
> Leave whatever things thou canst not
> Understand.
>
> Karl Rudolph Hagenbach

One great characteristic of holiness is never to be exacting, never to complain. Each complaint drags us down a degree in our upward course. If you would discern in whom God's spirit dwells, watch that person and notice whether you ever hear him murmur.

Gold Dust, Published 1880

When we wish things to be otherwise than they are, we lose sight of the great practical parts of the life of godliness. We wish, and wish, when, if we have done all that lies on us, we should fall quietly into the hands of God. Such wishing cuts the very sinews of our privileges and consolations. You are leaving me for a time, and you say that you wish you could leave me better or leave me with some assistance. But if it is right for you to go, it is right for me to meet what lies on me without a wish that I had less to meet or were better able to meet it.

Richard Cecil

He that is faithful in that which is least is faithful also in much. —Luke 16:10

The LORD preserveth the faithful. —Psalm 31:23

> The trivial round, the common task,
> Would furnish all we ought to ask;
> Room to deny ourselves; a road
> To bring us, daily, nearer God.
>
> John Keble

The endless retention of simple and exalted sentiments in obscure duties shapes the character to the disposition that will work with honor, if need be, in any tumult or hardship.

Ralph Waldo Emerson

Exactness in little duties is a wonderful source of cheerfulness.

Frederick William Faber

We are too fond of our own will. We want to be doing what we fancy are mighty things, but the great point is to do small things, when called to them, in a right spirit.

Richard Cecil

It is not on great occasions only that we are required to be faithful to the will of God. Occasions constantly occur, and we would be surprised to perceive how much our spiritual advancement depends on small obediences.

Madame Anne Sophie Swetchine

Strengthened with all might, according to his glorious power, unto all patience and longsuffering with joyfulness. —Colossians 1:11

God doth not need
Either man's works or His own gifts; who best
Bear His mild yoke, they serve Him best; His state
Is kingly; thousands at His bidding speed,
And post o'er land and ocean without rest;
They also serve who only stand and wait.

John Milton

*W*e cannot always be doing a great work, but we can always be doing something that belongs to our condition. To be silent, to suffer, to pray when we cannot act, is acceptable to God. A disappointment, a contradiction, a harsh word, an annoyance, a wrong received and endured as in His presence, is worth more than a long prayer. And we do not lose time if we bear its loss with gentleness and patience, provided the loss was inevitable and was not caused by our own fault.

Fénelon

Be not slothful, but followers of them who through faith and patience inherit the promises. —Hebrews 6:12

> Where now with pain thou treadest, trod
> The whitest of the saints of God!
> To show thee where their feet were set,
> The light which led them shineth yet.
>
> John Greenleaf Whittier

Let us learn from this communion of saints to live in hope. Those who are now at rest were once like ourselves. They were once weak, faulty, sinful. They had their burdens and hindrances, their slumbering and weariness, their failures and their falls. But now they have overcome. Their life was once homely and commonplace. Their day ran out as ours. Morning and noon and night came and went to them as to us. Their life, too, was as lonely and sad as yours. Little fretful circumstances and frequent disturbing changes wasted away their hours as yours. There is nothing in your life that was not in theirs. There was nothing in theirs but may be also in your own. They have overcome, one by one, each in his turn when the day came and God called him to the trial. And so will you likewise.

Cardinal Henry Edward Manning

Zebulun and Naphtali were a people that jeoparded their lives unto the death in the high places of the field.
—Judges 5:18

> Though Love repine, and Reason chafe,
> There came a voice without reply,
> 'T is man's perdition to be safe,
> When for the truth he ought to die.
>
> Ralph Waldo Emerson

Some say that the age of chivalry is past. The age of chivalry is never past, so long as there is a wrong left unredressed on earth, or a man or woman left to say, "I will redress that wrong, or spend my life in the attempt." The age of chivalry is never past, so long as we have faith enough to say, "God will help me to redress that wrong, or, if not me, He will help those who come after me, for His eternal will is to overcome evil with good."

Charles Kingsley

Thus man is made equal to every event. He can face danger for the right. A poor, tender, painful body he can run into flame or bullets or pestilence, with duty for his guide.

Ralph Waldo Emerson

*Let all those that put their trust in thee rejoice...let them
also that love thy name be joyful in thee.* —Psalm 5:11

He maketh me to lie down in green pastures.
—Psalm 23:2

I can hear these violets chorus
    To the sky's benediction above;
And we all are together lying
    On the bosom of Infinite Love.

Oh, the peace at the heart of Nature!
    Oh, the light that is not of day!
Why seek it afar forever,
    When it cannot be lifted away?
William Channing Gannett

*W*hat inexpressible joy for me, to look up
through the apple blossoms and the fluttering
leaves, and to see God's love there. What a joy to listen to the thrush that has built his nest among them
and to feel the love of God, who cares for the birds, in
every note that swells his little throat. What a joy to
look beyond to the bright blue depths of the sky and
feel they are a canopy of blessing, the roof of the
house of my Father. If clouds pass over it, it is the
unchangeable light they veil. Even when the day itself passes, I will see that the night itself only unveils
new worlds of light and know that if I could unwrap
fold after fold of God's universe, I should only unfold
more and more blessing, and see deeper and deeper
into the love that is at the heart of all.

Elizabeth Charles

June 1

One thing have I desired of the LORD, that will I seek after; that I may dwell in the house of the LORD all the days of my life, to behold the beauty of the LORD, and to inquire in his temple. —Psalm 27:4

Thy beauty, O my Father! All is Thine;
    But there is beauty in Thyself, from whence
The beauty Thou hast made doth ever flow
    In streams of never-failing affluence.

Thou art the Temple! and though I am lame,
    Lame from my birth and shall be till I die,
I enter through the Gate called Beautiful,
    And am alone with Thee, O Thou Most High!
               John White Chadwick

Consider that all which appears outwardly beautiful is solely derived from the invisible Spirit, which is the source of that external beauty. Then say joyfully, "Behold, these are streamlets from the uncreated Fountain. Behold, these are drops from the infinite Ocean of all good! Oh! how my inmost heart rejoices at the thought of that eternal, infinite Beauty, which is the source and origin of all created beauty!"

Lorenzo Scupoli

June 2

*We all, with open face beholding as in a glass the glory
of the Lord, are changed into the same image from
glory to glory, even as by the Spirit of the Lord.*
—2 Corinthians 3:18

> Then every tempting form of sin,
>   Shamed in Thy presence, disappears,
> And all the glowing, raptured soul
>   The likeness it contemplates wears.
>
> Philip Doddridge

A good man becomes the tabernacle of God, in which the divine Shechinah rests, and which the divine glory fills, when the frame of his mind and life is wholly according to that idea and pattern which he receives from the mount. We best glorify Him when we grow most like Him. We then act most for His glory when a true spirit of sanctity, justice, meekness, and so on, runs through all our actions. We act thus when we live in the world as those who converse with the great Mind and Wisdom of the whole world, with that almighty Spirit who made, supports, and governs all things, with that Being from whom all good flows and in whom there is no spot, stain, or shadow of evil. And so, being captivated and overcome by the sense of the divine loveliness and goodness, we endeavor to be like Him and conform ourselves, as much as may be, to Him.

Dr. John Smith

June 3

The righteous shall be glad in the LORD, and shall trust in him. —Psalm 64:10

Whoso trusteth in the LORD, happy is he.
—Proverbs 16:20

The heart that trusts forever sings,
And feels as light as it had wings,
A well of peace within it springs,
　　Come good or ill,
Whate'er today, tomorrow brings,
　　It is His will.

Isaac Williams

He will no longer weave a spotted life of shreds and patches, but he will live with a divine unity. He will cease from what is base and frivolous in his life and be content with all places, and with any service he can render. He will calmly confront the morrow in the liberty of that trust which carries God with it, and so has already the whole future in the bottom of the heart.

Ralph Waldo Emerson

He who believes in God is not careful for the morrow, but labors joyfully and with a great heart. *"He giveth his beloved* [as in] *sleep"* (Ps. 127:2). They must work and watch, yet never be careful or anxious. They must commit all to Him and live in serene tranquillity, with a quiet heart, as one who sleeps safely and quietly.

Martin Luther

Therefore, my beloved brethren, be ye stedfast, unmoveable, always abounding in the work of the Lord, forasmuch as ye know that your labour is not in vain in the Lord. —1 Corinthians 15:58

Say not, 'Twas all in vain,
    The anguish and the darkness and the strife;
Love thrown upon the waters comes again
    In quenchless yearnings for a nobler life.

Anna Shipton

Did you ever hear of a man who had striven all his life faithfully and singly toward an objective and in no measure obtained it? If a man constantly aspires, is he not elevated? Did ever a man try heroism, magnanimity, truth, sincerity, and find that there was no advantage in them, that it was a vain endeavor?

Henry David Thoreau

Do right, and God's recompense to you will be the power of doing more right. Give, and God's reward to you will be the spirit of giving more: a blessed spirit, for it is the Spirit of God Himself, whose life is the blessedness of giving. Love and God will pay you with the capacity of more love, for love is heaven. Love is God within you.

Frederick William Robertson

June 5

Speak, LORD; for thy servant heareth. —1 Samuel 3:9

> Though heralded with nought of fear,
>   Or outward sign or show:
> Though only to the inward ear
>   It whispers soft and low;
> Though dropping, as the manna fell,
>   Unseen, yet from above,
> Noiseless as dew-fall, heed it well,
>   Thy Father's call of love.
>
> John Greenleaf Whittier

One result of the attitude into which we are put by humility, by disinterestedness, by purity, by calmness, is that we have the opportunity, the disengagement, the silence, in which we may watch what is the will of God concerning us. If we think no more of ourselves than we ought to think, if we seek not our own but others' welfare, if we are prepared to take all things as God's dealings with us, then we may have a chance of catching from time to time what God has to tell us. In some cultures' devotions, one constant gesture is to put the hands to the ears, as if to listen for the messages from the other world. This is the attitude, the posture that our minds assume, if we have a standing place above and beyond the stir and confusion and dissipation of this mortal world.

Arthur Penrhyn Stanley

June 6

Him that overcometh will I make a pillar in the temple of my God. —Revelation 3:12

In whom ye also are builded together for an habitation of God through the Spirit. —Ephesians 2:22

None the place ordained refuseth,
They are one, and they are all,
Living stones, the Builder chooseth
For the courses of His wall.

Jean Ingelow

Slowly, through all the universe, that temple of God is being built. In any world, wherever a soul, by free-willed obedience, catches the fire of God's likeness, it is set into the growing walls, a living stone. When, in your hard fight, in your tiresome drudgery, or in your terrible temptation, you catch the purpose of your being and give yourself to God, and so give Him the chance to give Himself to you, your life, a living stone, is taken up and set into that growing wall. Wherever souls are being tried and ripened, in whatever commonplace and homely ways, there God is hewing out the pillars for His temple. Oh, if the stone can only have some vision of the temple of which it is to be a part forever, what patience must fill it as it feels the blows of the hammer and knows that success comes simply by letting itself be formed into whatever shape the Master wills.

Phillips Brooks

June 7

Ye are all the children of light, and the children of the day. —1 Thessalonians 5:5

Light is sown for the righteous, and gladness for the upright in heart. —Psalm 97:11

Serene will be our days and bright
And happy will our nature be,
When love is an unerring light,
And joy its own security.
William Wordsworth

*N*othing can produce so great a serenity of life as a mind free from guilt and kept untainted, not only from actions, but purposes that are wicked. By this means the soul will be not only unpolluted but also undisturbed. The fountain will run clear and unsullied. The streams that flow from it will be just and honest deeds, ecstasies of satisfaction, a brisk energy of spirit, which makes a man an enthusiast in his joy, and a tenacious memory, sweeter than hope. For as shrubs that are cut down with the morning dew upon them do for a long time after retain their fragrance, so the good actions of a wise man perfume his mind and leave a rich scent behind them. So that joy is, as it were, watered with these essences, and owes its flourishing to them.

Plutarch

June 8

Who hath despised the day of small things?
—Zechariah 4:10

Little things
On little wings
Bear little souls to heaven.

Anonymous

*A*n occasional effort even of an ordinary holiness may accomplish great acts of sacrifice or bear severe pressure of extraordinary trial, especially if it is the subject of observation. The true saintly beauty of the spirit is found in constant discipline, though unnoticed, and in silent unselfishness that becomes the hidden habit of life. This is the result of care and lowly love in little things. Perfection is attained most readily by this constancy of religious faithfulness in all minor details of life, consecrating the daily efforts of self-forgetting love.

Thomas Thelluson Carter

Love's secret is to be always doing things for God, and not to mind because they are such very little things.

Frederick William Faber

There may be living and habitual conversation in heaven, under the aspect of the most simple, ordinary life. Let us always remember that holiness does not consist in doing uncommon things but in doing everything with purity of heart.

Cardinal Henry Edward Manning

June 9

He that is slow to anger is better than the mighty; and
he that ruleth his spirit than he that taketh a city.
—Proverbs 16:32

Purge from our hearts the stains so deep and foul,
    Of wrath and pride and care;
Send Thine own holy calm upon the soul,
    And bid it settle there!

Anonymous

*L*et this truth be present to you in the excitement of anger: that to be moved by passion is not manly, but that mildness and gentleness, since they are more agreeable to human nature, are also more manly. For in the same degree in which a man's mind is nearer to freedom from all passion, in the same degree also is it nearer to strength.

Marcus Aurelius Antoninus

It is no great matter to associate with the good and gentle. This is naturally pleasing to all, and everyone willingly enjoys peace, and loves those best who agree with him. But to be able to live peaceably with hard and perverse persons, or with the disorderly, or with those who go contrary to us, is a great grace and a most commendable and manly thing.

Thomas à Kempis

Who is among you that feareth the LORD, that obeyeth the voice of his servant, that walketh in darkness, and hath no light? let him trust in the name of the LORD, and stay upon his God. —Isaiah 50:10

The LORD my God will enlighten my darkness.
—Psalm 18:28

When we in darkness walk,
Nor feel the heavenly flame,
Then is the time to trust our God,
And rest upon His name.
Augustus Montague Toplady

*H*e has a special tenderness of love towards you because you are in the dark and have no light, and His heart is glad when you do arise and say, "I will go to my Father." For He sees you through all the gloom through which you cannot see Him. Say to Him, "My God, I am very dull and low and hard, but You are wise and high and tender, and You are my God. I am Your child. Forsake me not." Then fold the arms of your faith, and wait in quietness until light goes up in the darkness. Fold the arms of your faith, I say, but not of your action. Remember something that you ought to do, and go and do it, if it is but the sweeping of a room or the preparing of a meal or a visit to a friend. Heed not your feelings; do your work.

George MacDonald

June 11

In the day when I cried thou answeredst me, and strengthenedst me with strength in my soul.
—Psalm 138:3

It is not that I feel less weak, but Thou
Wilt be my strength; it is not that I see
Less sin; but more of pardoning love with Thee,
    And all-sufficient grace. Enough! And now
All fluttering thought is stilled; I only rest,
And feel that Thou art near, and know that I am blest.
                    Frances Ridley Havergal

Yes, though you cannot believe, do not be dismayed at that. Only sink into, or at least pant after, the hidden measure of life, which is not in that which distresses, disturbs, and fills you with thoughts, fears, troubles, anguish, darkness, terrors, and the like. No, no! Sink into that which inclines to the patience, to the stillness, to the hope, to the waiting, to the silence before the Father.
                    Isaac Penington

We have only to be patient, to pray, and to do His will, according to our present light and strength, and the growth of the soul will go on. The plant grows in the mist and under clouds as truly as under sunshine. So does the heavenly principle within.
                    William Ellery Channing

For whatsoever is born of God overcometh the world: and this is the victory that overcometh the world, even our faith. —1 John 5:4

One holy Church, one army strong,
  One steadfast high intent,
One working band, one harvest-song,
  One King omnipotent.

Samuel Johnson

*W*e listened to a man whom we felt to be, with all his heart and soul and strength, striving against whatever was mean and unmanly and unrighteous in our little world. It was not the cold, clear voice of one giving advice and warning from serene heights to those who were struggling and sinning below. But it was the warm, living voice of one who was fighting for us and by our sides, and calling on us to help him and ourselves and one another. And so, wearily and little by little, but surely and steadily on the whole, was brought home to the young boy, for the first time, the meaning of his life. He learned that it was no fool's or sluggard's paradise into which he had wandered by chance, but a battlefield ordained from of old, where there are no spectators. And the youngest must choose his side, and the stakes are life and death.

Thomas Hughes

If we walk in the light, as he is in the light, we have fellowship one with another. —1 John 1:7

God is not unrighteous to forget your work and labour of love, which ye have showed toward his name, in that ye have ministered to the saints, and do minister.
—Hebrews 6:10

Wherever in the world I am,
In whatsoe'er estate,
I have a fellowship with hearts,
To keep and cultivate,
And a work of lowly love to do
For the Lord on whom I wait.
Anna Laetitia Waring

*W*e do not always perceive that even the writing of a note of congratulation, the fabrication of something intended as an offering of affection, our necessary dealings with characters who have no congeniality with our own, or hours apparently trifled away in the domestic circle, may be made by us the performance of a most sacred and blessed work. It may even be the carrying out, after our feeble measure, of the design of God for the increase of happiness.

Anna, or *Passages from Home Life*

Definite work is not always that which is cut and squared for us, but that which comes as a claim upon the conscience, whether it's nursing in a hospital or hemming a handkerchief.

Elizabeth M. Sewell

June 14

The LORD shall give thee rest from thy sorrow, and from thy fear, and from the hard bondage wherein thou wast made to serve. —Isaiah 14:3

Today, beneath Thy chastening eye,
I crave alone for peace and rest;
Submissive in Thy hand to lie,
    And feel that it is best.
John Greenleaf Whittier

O Lord, You are *"as the shadow of a great rock in a weary land"* (Isa. 32:2), who beholds Your weak creatures weary of labor, weary of pleasure, weary of hope deferred, weary of self. In Your abundant compassion, and unutterable tenderness, bring us, I pray You, unto Your rest. Amen.
Christina G. Rossetti

Grant to me, above all things that can be desired, to rest in You and in You to have my heart at peace. You are the true peace of the heart. You are its only rest. Out of You all things are hard and restless. In this very peace, that is, in You, the One Chiefest Eternal Good, I will sleep and rest. Amen.
Thomas à Kempis

You have made us for Yourself, O Lord, and our hearts are restless until they rest in You.
St. Augustine

June 15

God is our refuge and strength, a very present help in trouble. Therefore will not we fear, though the earth be removed, and though the mountains be carried into the midst of the sea. —Psalm 46:1–2

Though waves and storms go o'er my head,
    Though strength and health and friends be gone,
Though joys be withered all, and dead,
    Though every comfort be withdrawn,
On this my steadfast soul relies,
    Father! Thy mercy never dies.

Johann Andreas Röthe

Your external circumstances may change. Toil may take the place of rest. You may have sickness instead of health. Trials may thicken within and without. Externally you are the prey of such circumstances, but if your heart is stayed on God, no changes or chances can touch it. All that may befall you will but draw you closer to Him. Whatever the present moment may bring, your knowledge that it is His will and that your future heavenly life will be influenced by it, will make all not only tolerable, but as a welcome to you. No unpredictable changes can affect you greatly, knowing that He who holds you in His powerful hand cannot change, but abides forever.

Jean Nicolas Grou

June 16

Now unto him that is able to do exceeding abundantly above all that we ask or think, according to the power that worketh in us, unto him be glory in the church by Christ Jesus throughout all ages, world without end. Amen. —Ephesians 3:20–21

> We would not meager gifts down-call
> When Thou dost yearn to yield us all;
> But for this life, this little hour,
> Ask all Thy love and care and power.
>
> Jean Ingelow

God so loves us that He would make all things channels to us and messengers of His love. Do for His sake deeds of love, and He will give you His love. Still yourself, your own cares, your own thoughts for Him, and He will speak to your heart. Ask for Himself, and He will give you Himself. Truly, the love of God is a secret hidden thing, known only to those who seek it. For what man can have here of God's love is only slight a foretaste of the endless ocean of His love!

Edward B. Pusey

June 17

Consider the lilies of the field, how they grow.
—Matthew 6:28

> They do not toil:
> Content with their allotted task
> They do but grow; they do not ask
> A richer lot, a higher sphere,
> But in their loveliness appear,
> And grow, and smile, and do their best,
> And unto God they leave the rest.
>
> Marianne Farningham

*I*nterpose no barrier to His mighty life-giving power, working in you all the good pleasure of His will. Yield yourself up utterly to His sweet control. Put your growing into His hands as completely as you have put all your other affairs. Allow Him to manage it as He will. Do not concern yourself about it or even think of it. Trust Him absolutely and always. Accept each moment's dispensation as it comes to you from His dear hands, as being the needed sunshine or dew for that moment's growth. Say a continual "yes" to your Father's will.

Hannah Whitall Smith

Your own self-will and anxiety, your hurry and labor, disturb your peace and prevent Me from working in you. Look at the little flowers in the serene summer days; they quietly open their petals, and the sun shines into them with his gentle influences. So will I do for you, if you will yield yourself to Me.

Gerhard Tersteegen

Wherefore, if God so clothe the grass of the field, which to day is, and to morrow is cast into the oven, shall he not much more clothe you, O ye of little faith?
—Matthew 6:30

I trust in the mercy of God for ever and ever.
—Psalm 52:8

Calmly we look behind us, on joys and sorrows past,
We know that all is mercy now, and shall be well at last;
Calmly we look before us,—we fear no future ill,
Enough for safety and for peace, if Thou art with us still.
Jane Borthwick

Neither go back in fear and misgiving to the past, nor in anxiety and forecasting to the future, but lie quiet under His hand, having no will but His.

Cardinal Henry Edward Manning

I saw a delicate flower had grown up two feet high, between the horses' path and the wheel track. An inch more to right or left had sealed its fate, or an inch higher. Yet it lived to flourish as much as if it had a thousand acres of untrodden space around it and never knew the danger it incurred. It did not borrow nor invite an evil fate by anticipating it.

Henry David Thoreau

June 19

The LORD shall preserve thee from all evil: he shall pre-
serve thy soul. —Psalm 121:7

Under Thy wings my God, I rest,
Under Thy shadow safely lie;
By Thy own strength in peace possessed,
While dreaded evils pass me by.

Anna Laetitia Waring

A heart rejoicing in God delights in all His will and is surely provided with the firmest joy in all estates. For if nothing can come to pass beside or against His will, then that soul cannot be vexed which delights in Him and has no will but His, but follows Him in all times, in all estates, not only when He shines brightly on them, but also when they are clouded. That flower which follows the sun does so even in dark and cloudy days when it does not shine forth, yet it follows the hidden course and motion of it. So the soul that moves after God keeps that course even when He hides His face. It is content, yes, even glad at His will in all estates or conditions or events.

Robert Leighton

Let God do with me what He will, anything He will, whatever it is. It will be either heaven itself or some beginning of it.

William Mountford

Be merciful unto me: for my soul trusteth in thee: yea, in the shadow of thy wings will I make my refuge, until these calamities be overpast. —Psalm 57:1

My God! in whom are all the springs
Of boundless love and grace unknown,
Hide me beneath Thy spreading wings,
Till the dark cloud is overblown.

Isaac Watts

*I*n time of trouble do not go out of yourself to seek for aid, for the whole benefit of trial consists in silence, patience, rest, and resignation. In this condition divine strength is found for the hard warfare, because God Himself fights for the soul.

Miguel Molinos

In vain you will let your mind run out after help in times of trouble. It is like putting to sea in a storm. Sit still, and search out your principles. If you find none that furnish you with somewhat of a stay and prop, and that point you to quietness and silent submission, depend upon it you have never yet learned truth from the Spirit of Truth, whatever notions thereof you may have picked up from this or another description of it.

Mary Anne Kelty

June 21

Thou calledst in trouble, and I delivered thee.
—Psalm 81:7

Be strong, and of good courage; dread not, nor be dismayed. —1 Chronicles 22:13

Thou canst calm the troubled mind,
Thou its dread canst still;
Teach me to be all resigned
To my Father's will.

Heinrich Puchta

*T*hough this patient, meek resignation is to be exercised with regard to all outward things and occurrences of life, it chiefly relates to our own inward state, the troubles, perplexities, weaknesses, and disorders of our own souls. And to stand turned to a patient, meek, humble resignation to God, when your own impatience, wrath, pride, and irresignation attack yourself, is a higher and more beneficial performance of this duty, than when you stand turned to meekness and patience, when attacked by the pride or wrath or disorderly passions of other people.

William Law

*There hath no temptation taken you but such as is
common to man: but God is faithful, who will not suffer
you to be tempted above that ye are able; but will with
the temptation also make a way to escape, that ye may
be able to bear it.* —1 Corinthians 10:13

> Not so, not so, no load of woe
> Need bring despairing frown;
> For while we bear it, we can bear,
> Past that, we lay it down.
> Sarah Williams

*E*verything that happens, either happens in such
a way that you are formed by nature to bear it,
or that you are not formed by nature to bear it. If,
then, it happens to you in such way that you are
formed by nature to bear it, do not complain but
bear it as you are formed by nature to bear it. But, if
it happens in such a way that you are not able to
bear it, do not complain, for it will perish after it has
consumed you. Remember, however, that you are
formed by nature to bear everything, with respect to
that which depends on your own opinion to make it
endurable and tolerable, by thinking that it is either
your interest or your duty to do this.

Marcus Aurelius Antoninus

Why art thou cast down, O my soul? and why art thou disquieted within me? hope thou in God: for I shall yet praise him, who is the health of my countenance, and my God. —Psalm 42:11

Ah! why by passing clouds oppressed,
Should vexing thought distract thy breast!
Turn thou to Him in every pain,
Whom never suppliant sought in vain;
Thy strength in joy's ecstatic day,
Thy hope, when joy has passed away.

Henry Francis Lyte

*B*eware of letting your care degenerate into anxiety and unrest, tossed as you are amid the winds and waves of sundry troubles. Keep your eyes fixed on the Lord, and say, "Oh, my God, I look to You alone. Be my guide, my pilot," and then be comforted. When the shore is gained, who will heed the toil and the storm? And we will steer safely through every storm, as long as our heart is right, our intention fervent, our courage steadfast, and our trust fixed on God. If at times we are somewhat stunned by the tempest, never fear. Let us take a breath and go on afresh. Do not be disconcerted by the fits of vexation and uneasiness that are sometimes produced by the multiplicity of your domestic worries. No indeed, dearest child, all these are but opportunities of strengthening yourself in the loving, forbearing graces that our dear Lord sets before us.

Francis de Sales

June 24

Even so, Father: for so it seemed good in thy sight.
        —Matthew 11:26

Let nothing make thee sad or fretful,
        Or too regretful;
                Be still;
What God hath ordered must be right,
Then find in it thine own delight,
                My will.

                                Paul Flemming

If we listen to our self-love, we will consider our lot less by what it is than by what it is not. We will dwell on its hindrances and be blind to its possibilities and compare it only with imaginary lives. We will indulge in flattering dreams of what we should do, if we had the power, and give, if we had the wealth, and be, if we had no temptations. We will be forever querulously pleading our difficulties and privations as excuses for our unloving temper and unfruitful life, and fancying ourselves injured beings, virtually frowning at the dear Providence who loves us and chafing with a self-torture that invites no pity. If we yield ourselves to God and sincerely accept our lot as assigned by Him, we will count up its contents and disregard its omissions. And, be it as feeble as a cripple's and as narrow as a child's, we will find in it resources of good, surpassing our best economy, and sacred claims that may keep awake our highest will.

                                James Martineau

June 25

My times are in thy hand. —Psalm 31:15

Every purpose of the LORD shall be performed.
                —Jeremiah 51:29

I am so glad! It is such rest to know
That Thou hast ordered and appointed all,
And wilt yet order and appoint my lot.
For though so much I cannot understand,
And would not choose, has been, and yet may be,
Thou choosest, Thou performest, Thou, my Lord.
This is enough for me.

                              Frances Ridley Havergal

We mustn't be in a hurry to settle and choose our own lot. We must wait to be guided. We are led on, like the little children, by a way that we do not know. It is a vain thought to flee from the work that God appoints for us, for the sake of finding a greater blessing to our own souls, as if we could choose for ourselves where we will find the fullness of the Divine Presence, instead of seeking it where alone it is to be found, in loving obedience.

                              George Eliot

Everywhere and at all times it is in your power piously to acquiesce in your present condition, and to behave justly to those who are about you.

                              Marcus Aurelius Antoninus

And when ye stand praying, forgive, if ye have ought against any: that your Father also which is in heaven may forgive you your trespasses. But if ye do not forgive, neither will your Father which is in heaven forgive your trespasses. —Mark 11:25–26

> 'T is not enough to weep my sins,
> 'T is but one step to heaven:
> When I am kind to others,—then
> I know myself forgiven.
>
> Frederick William Faber

*E*very relation to mankind, of hate or scorn or neglect, is full of vexation and torment. There is nothing to do with men but to love them, to contemplate their virtues with admiration, their faults with pity and forbearance, and their injuries with forgiveness. Burden all the ingenuity of your mind to devise some other things, but you never can find it. To hate your adversary will not help you. To kill him will not help you. Nothing within the compass of the universe can help you, but to love him. But let that love flow out upon everyone around you, and what could harm you? How many a knot of mystery and misunderstanding would be untied by one word spoken in simple and confiding truth of heart! How many a solitary place would be made glad if love were there, and how many a dark dwelling would be filled with light!

Orville Dewey

June 27

The kingdom of God is within you. —Luke 17:21

Oh, take this heart that I would give
Forever to be all Thine own;
I to myself no more would live,
Come, Lord, be Thou my King alone.
Gerhard Tersteegen

*H*erein is the work assigned to the individual
soul: to have life in itself; to make our sphere,
whatever it is, sufficient for a reign of God within
ourselves, for a true and full reign of our Father's
abounding spirit. We should be thankful, unuttera-
bly thankful, if, with the place and the companion-
ship assigned to us, we are permitted to build an
earthly tabernacle of grace and goodness and holy
love, a home like a temple. However, should this be
denied us, we should be resolved, for our own souls,
that God will reign there, for ourselves at least that
we will not, by sin or disobedience or impious distrust, break with our own wills our filial connection
with our Father. We should do all this whether joyful or sorrowing, struggling with the perplexity and
foulness of circumstance, or in an atmosphere of
peace. Whether in dear fellowship or alone, our desire and prayer will be that God may have in us a
realm where His will is law, and where obedience
and submission spring, not from calculating pru-
dence or ungodly fear, but from communion of
spirit, ever humble aspiration, and ever loving trust.
John Hamilton Thom

June 28

The LORD preserveth the simple. —Psalm 116:6

> Thy home is with the humble, Lord!
>   The simple are Thy rest;
> Thy lodging is in childlike hearts;
>   Thou makest there Thy nest.
>
> Frederick William Faber

*T*his deliverance of the soul from all useless and selfish and unquiet cares brings to it an unspeakable peace and freedom. This is true simplicity. This state of entire resignation and perpetual acquiescence produces true liberty, and this liberty brings perfect simplicity. The soul that knows no self-seeking, no interested ends, is thoroughly candid. It goes straight forward without hindrance. Its path opens daily more and more to *"perfect day"* (Prov. 4:18), in proportion as its self-renunciation and its self-forgetfulness increase. And its peace, amid whatever troubles beset it, will be as boundless as the depths of the sea.

Fénelon

Let not him that girdeth on his harness boast himself as he that putteth it off. —1 Kings 20:11

Put on the whole armour of God. —Ephesians 6:11

Was I not girded for the battlefield?
Bore I not helm of pride and glittering sword?
Behold the fragments of my broken shield,
And lend to me Thy heavenly armor, Lord!

Anonymous

Oh, be at least able to say in that day, "Lord, I am no hero. I have been careless, cowardly, sometimes all but mutinous. Punishment I have deserved, I do not deny it. But a traitor I have never been. A deserter I have never been. I have tried to fight on Your side in Your battle against evil. I have tried to do the duty that lay nearest me, and to leave whatever You committed to my charge a little better than I found it. I have not been good, but I have at least tried to be good. Take the will for the deed, good Lord. Do not strike my unworthy name off the roll call of the noble and victorious army, which is the blessed company of all faithful people. And let me, too, be found written in the Book of Life, even though I stand the lowest and last upon its list. Amen."

Charles Kingsley

And the work of righteousness shall be peace; and the effect of righteousness quietness and assurance for ever.
—Isaiah 32:17

> The heart that ministers for Thee
> In Thy own work will rest;
> And the subject spirit of a child
> Can serve Thy children best.
>
> Anna Laetitia Waring

*I*t does not matter where or what we are, as long as we are His servants. They are happy who have wide field and great strength to fulfill His mission of compassion. They, too, are blessed who, in sheltered homes and narrow ways of duty, wait upon Him in lowly services of love. Wise or simple, gifted or limited in knowledge, in the world's gaze or in hidden paths, high or low, encompassed by affections and joys of home or lonely and content in God alone, what matters, as long as they bear the seal of the living God? Blessed company, unknown to each other, unknowing even themselves!

Cardinal Henry Edward Manning

July 1

And in the morning, then ye shall see the glory of the
LORD. —Exodus 16:7

Serving the Lord; rejoicing in hope.
—Romans 12:11–12

Every day is a fresh beginning,
Every morn is the world made new.
You who are weary of sorrow and sinning,
Here is a beautiful hope for you;
A hope for me and a hope for you.

Susan Coolidge

*B*e patient with everyone, but above all with yourself. I mean, do not be disturbed because of your imperfections, and always rise up bravely from a fall. I am glad that you daily make a new beginning. There is no better means of progress in the spiritual life than to be continually beginning afresh, and never to think that we have done enough.

Francis de Sales

Because perseverance is so difficult, even when supported by the grace of God, from that is the value of new beginnings. For new beginnings are the life of perseverance.

Edward B. Pusey

Herein do I exercise myself, to have always a conscience void of offence toward God, and toward men.
—Acts 24:16

I will instruct thee and teach thee in the way which thou shalt go: I will guide thee with mine eye.
—Psalm 32:8

Oh, keep thy conscience sensitive;
No inward token miss;
And go where grace entices thee;
Perfection lies in this.

Frederick William Faber

We need only to obey. There is guidance for each of us, and by lowly listening we will hear the right word.

Ralph Waldo Emerson

The heights of Christian perfection can only be reached by each moment faithfully following the Guide who is to lead you there. And He reveals your way to you one step at a time, in the little things of your daily lives, asking only on your part that you yield yourselves up to His guidance. If, then, in anything you feel doubtful or troubled, be sure that it is the voice of your Lord, and surrender at once to His bidding, rejoicing with a great joy that He has begun thus to lead and guide you.

Hannah Whitall Smith

July 3

He shall redeem Israel from all his iniquities.
    —Psalm 130:8

Be it according to Thy word;
    Redeem me from all sin;
My heart would now receive Thee, Lord,
    Come in, my Lord, come in!
                                    Charles Wesley

When you wake, or as soon as you are dressed, offer up your whole self to God, soul and body, thoughts and purposes and desires, to be for that day what He wills. Think of the occasions of the sin likely to befall you, and go, as a child, to your Father who is in heaven. Tell Him your trials in some such simple and childlike words as these: "You know good Lord, that I am tempted to [*then name the temptations, and the ways in which you sin, as well as you know them*]. But, good Lord, for love of You, I would this day keep wholly from all [*naming the sin*] and be very [*naming the opposite grace*]. I will not by Your grace, do one [*naming the act*] or speak one [*naming the type of*] word, or give one [*naming the*] look, or harbor one [*naming the*] thought in my soul. If You allow any of these temptations to come upon me this day, I desire to think, speak, and do only what You will. Lord, without You I can do nothing; with You I can do all."
                                    Edward B. Pusey

*Remember, O LORD, thy tender mercies and thy lov-
ingkindnesses; for they have been ever of old.*
—Psalm 25:6

My Father! see
I trust the faithfulness displayed of old,
I trust the love that never can grow cold
I trust in Thee.

Christian Intelligencer

*B*e not so much discouraged in the sight of what
is yet to be done, as comforted in His goodwill
towards you. It is true, He has chastened you with
rods and sore afflictions, but did He ever take away
His loving-kindness from you? Or did His faithfulness ever fail in the sorest, blackest, thickest, darkest night that ever befell you?

Isaac Penington

We call Him the "God of our fathers," and we
feel that there is some stability at the center. We
can tell our cares to the One listening at our right
hand, by whom these cares are remembered and
removed.

James Martineau

July 5

He stayeth his rough wind in the day of the east wind.
—Isaiah 27:8

A bruised reed shall he not break. —Isaiah 42:3

All my life I still have found,
 And I will forget it never;
Every sorrow hath its bound,
 And no cross endures forever.
All things else have but their day,
God's love only lasts for aye.

Paul Gerhardt

*W*e never have more than we can bear. The present hour we are always able to endure. As our day is, so is our strength. If the trials of many years were gathered into one, they would overwhelm us. Therefore, in pity to our little strength, He sends first one, then another, then removes both and lays on a third, heavier, perhaps, than either. But, all is so wisely measured to our strength that the bruised reed is never broken. We do not look enough at our trials in this continuous and successive view. Each one is sent to teach us something, and altogether they have a lesson that is beyond the power of any to teach alone.

Cardinal Henry Edward Manning

July 6

I the LORD have called thee in righteousness, and will hold thine hand, and will keep thee. —Isaiah 42:6

O keep my soul, and deliver me: let me not be ashamed; for I put my trust in thee. —Psalm 25:20

> I do not ask my cross to understand,
>> My way to see;
> Better in darkness just to feel Thy hand,
>> And follow Thee.
>
> Adelaide Anne Procter

O Lord, if only my will may remain right and firm towards You, do with me whatever will please You. For it cannot be anything but good, whatever You will do with me. If it is Your will I should be in darkness, may You be blessed. If it is Your will I should be in light, may You again be blessed. If You deign to comfort me, may You be blessed. If You will have me afflicted, may You be equally blessed. O Lord, for Your sake I will cheerfully suffer whatever will come on me with Your permission.

Thomas à Kempis

My soul could not incline itself on the one side or the other, since another will had taken the place of its own, but only nourished itself with the daily providences of God.

Madame Jeanne Guyon

The LORD is my light and my salvation; whom shall I fear? the LORD is the strength of my life; of whom shall I be afraid? —Psalm 27:1

Thou hidden Source of calm repose,
    Thou all-sufficient Love divine,
My Help and Refuge from my foes,
    Secure I am while Thou art mine:
And lo! from sin, and grief, and shame,
I hide me, Father, in Thy name.

Charles Wesley

*W*hatever troubles come on you—of mind, body, or estate, from within or from without, from chance or from intent, from friends or foes— whatever your trouble is, though you are lonely, oh, children of a heavenly Father, do not be afraid!

Cardinal John Henry Newman

Whatever befalls you, do not receive it from the hand of any creature, but from Him alone. Render back all to Him, seeking in all things His pleasure and honor, the purifying and subduing of yourself. What can harm you, when all must first touch God, within whom you have enclosed yourself?

Robert Leighton

How God rejoices over a soul, which, surrounded on all sides by suffering and misery, does upon earth what the angels do in heaven, namely, loves, adores, and praises God!

Gerhard Tersteegen

And be ye kind one to another. —Ephesians 4:32

> She doeth little kindnesses
>> Which most leave undone or despise;
> For nought which sets one heart at ease,
> And giveth happiness or peace,
>> Is low-esteemed in her eyes.
>
> James Russell Lowell

What was the secret of such a one's power? What had she done? Absolutely nothing. But radiant smiles, beaming good-humor, the tact of divining what everyone felt and everyone wanted, told that she had got out of self and learned to think of others. At one time, her selflessness showed itself in playing down the quarrel, which lowering brows and raised tones already showed to be impending, by sweet words. At another, it showed by smoothing an invalid's pillow. At another, it showed by soothing a sobbing child. At another, by humoring and softening a father who had returned weary and ill-tempered from the irritating cares of business. None but she saw those things. None but a loving heart could see them. That was the secret of her heavenly power. The one who will be found in trial capable of great acts of love is ever the one who is always doing considerate small ones.

Frederick William Robertson

Love is of God; and every one that loveth is born of God, and knoweth God. —1 John 4:7

Oh, might we all our lineage prove,
Give and forgive, do good and love;
By soft endearments, in kind strife,
Lightening the load of daily life.

John Keble

We may, if we choose, make the worst of one another. Everyone has his weak points. Everyone has his faults. We may make the worst of these. We may fix our attention constantly upon these. But we may also make the best of one another. We may forgive, even as we hope to be forgiven. We may put ourselves in the place of others and ask what we should wish to be done to us, and thought of us, were we in their place. By loving whatever is lovable in those around us, love will flow back from them to us, and life will become a pleasure instead of a pain. Earth will become like heaven, and we will become worthy followers of Him whose name is Love.

Arthur Penrhyn Stanley

July 10

*The LORD will perfect that which concerneth me: thy
mercy, O LORD, endureth for ever: forsake not the works
of thine own hands.* —Psalm 138:8

As God leads me, will I go,
　　Nor choose my way;
Let Him choose the joy or woe
　　Of every day:
They cannot hurt my soul,
Because in His control:
I leave to Him the whole,—
　　His children may.

Lampertus Gedicke

*W*hy is it that we are so busy with the future? It
is not our province. Is there not a criminal
interference with Him to whom it belongs in our
feverish, anxious attempts to dispose of it, and in
filling it up with shadows of good and evil shaped by
our own wild imaginations? Our duty and our happiness is to do God's will as fast as it is made known
to us. We should inquire hourly—I had almost said
each moment—what He requires of us, and leave
ourselves, our friends, and every interest at His control, with a cheerful trust that the path that He
marks out leads to our perfection and to Himself.
And, why will we not walk in the plain, simple way?

William Ellery Channing

When he giveth quietness, who then can make trouble?
—Job 34:29

None of these things move me. —Acts 20:24

> I've many a cross to take up now,
>   And many left behind;
> But present troubles move me not,
>   Nor shake my quiet mind.
> And what may be tomorrow's cross
>   I never seek to find;
> My Father says, "Leave that to me,
>   And keep a quiet mind."

Anonymous

Let us then think only of the present and not even permit our minds to wander with curiosity into the future. The future is not yet ours. Perhaps it never will be. It is exposing ourselves to temptation to wish to anticipate God and to prepare ourselves for things that He may not destine for us. If such things should come to pass, He will give us light and strength according to the need. Why should we desire to meet difficulties prematurely when we have neither strength nor light as yet provided for them? Let us give heed to the present, whose duties are pressing. It is fidelity to the present that prepares us for fidelity in the future.

Fénelon

Every hour comes with some little bundle of God's will fastened upon its back.

Frederick William Faber

*Be strong and of a good courage, fear not, nor be afraid
of them: for the LORD thy God, he it is that doth go with
thee; he will not fail thee, nor forsake thee.*
—Deuteronomy 31:6

The timid it concerns to ask their way,
And fear what foe in caves and swamps can stray,
To make no step until the event is known,
And ills to come as evils past bemoan.
Not so the wise; no coward watch he keeps
To spy what danger on his pathway creeps;
Go where he will, the wise man is at home,
His hearth the earth,—his hall the azure dome;
Where his clear spirit leads him, there's his road,
By God's own light illumined and foreshowed.

Ralph Waldo Emerson

*T*hough I sympathize, I do not share in the least
the feeling of being disheartened and cast
down. It is not things of this sort that depress me,
or ever will. The contrary things, praise, openings,
the feeling of the greatness of my work, and my in-
ability in relation to it—these things oppress and
cast me down. But little hindrances and closing up
of accustomed or expected avenues and the presence
of difficulties to be overcome—I'm not going to be
cast down by trifles such as these.

James Hinton

And the LORD shall guide thee continually, and satisfy thy soul in drought. —Isaiah 58:11

> Wherever He may guide me,
>   No want shall turn me back;
> My Shepherd is beside me,
>   And nothing can I lack.
> His wisdom ever waketh,
>   His sight is never dim,
> He knows the way He taketh,
>   And I will walk with Him.

Anna Laetitia Waring

*A*bandon yourself to His care and guidance as a sheep in the care of a shepherd, and trust Him utterly. It is no matter that you may seem to yourself to be in the very midst of a desert, with nothing green about you, inwardly or outwardly. You may think you will have to make a long journey before you can get into the green pastures. But our Shepherd will turn that very place where you are into green pastures, for He has power to make the desert rejoice and blossom as a rose.

Hannah Whitall Smith

*Be not conformed to this world: but be ye transformed
by the renewing of your mind.* —Romans 12:2

> Father, let our faithful mind
> Rest, on Thee alone inclined;
> Every anxious thought repress,
> Keep our souls in perfect peace.
>
> Charles Wesley

Some of the steps that lead to obedience to the holy precept in our text are the following: retirement from anxieties of every kind; entering into no disputes; avoiding all frivolous talk; simplifying everything we engage in, whether in a way of doing or suffering; denying the imagination its false activities, and the intellect its false searchings after what it cannot obtain.

James Pierrepoint Greaves

Retire inwardly. Wait to feel something of God's Spirit, discovering and drawing away from that which is contrary to His holy nature, and leading into that which is acceptable to Him. As the mind is joined to this, some true light and life are received.

Isaac Penington

Act faithfully to your convictions, and when you have been unfaithful, bear with yourself and resume always with calm simplicity your little task. Suppress, as much as you possibly can, all recurrence to yourself, and you will suppress much vanity. Accustom yourself to much calmness and an indifference to events.

Madame Jeanne Guyon

Lift up your heads, O ye gates; even lift them up, ye everlasting doors; and the King of glory shall come in.
—Psalm 24:9

Ye are the temple of the living God.
—2 Corinthians 6:16

Fling wide the portals of your heart,
Make it a temple set apart
From earthly use for Heaven's employ,
Adorned with prayer, and love, and joy.
So shall your Sovereign enter in,
And new and nobler life begin.

Georg Weissel

You should know that your soul is the center, habitation, and kingdom of God. Therefore, so that the sovereign King may rest on that throne of your soul, you ought to take pains to keep it clean, quiet, and peaceable. It should be clean from guilt and defects, quiet from fears, and peaceable in temptations and tribulations. You ought always, then, to keep your heart in peace, so that you may keep pure that temple of God. And, with a right and pure intention you are to work, pray, obey, and suffer, without being in the least moved, whatever it pleases the Lord to send to you.

Miguel Molinos

Oh how great is thy goodness, which thou hast laid up for them that fear thee; which thou hast wrought for them that trust in thee. —Psalm 31:19

I will sing unto the LORD, because he hath dealt bountifully with me. —Psalm 13:6

Thy calmness bends serene above
    My restlessness to still;
Around me flows Thy quickening life,
    To nerve my faltering will;
Thy presence fills my solitude;
Thy providence turns all to good.

Samuel Longfellow

*W*ith a heart devoted to God and full of God, no longer seek Him in the heavens above or the earth beneath or in the things under the earth. Recognize Him as the great fact of the universe, separate from no place or part, but revealed in all places and in all things and events, moment by moment. And as eternity alone will exhaust this momentary revelation, which has sometimes been called the "eternal now," you will thus find God ever present and ever new. Your soul will adore Him and feed upon Him in the things and events that each new moment brings. You will never be absent from Him, and He will never be absent from you.

Thomas Cogswell Upham

July 17

For I reckon that the sufferings of this present time are not worthy to be compared with the glory which shall be revealed in us. —Romans 8:18

The power of an endless life. —Hebrews 7:16

> Believ'st thou in eternal things?
>   Thou knowest, in thy inmost heart,
> Thou art not clay; thy soul hath wings,
>   And what thou seest is but part.
> Make this thy med'cine for the smart
>   Of every day's distress; be dumb,
> In each new loss thou truly art
>   Tasting the power of things that come.
>
> Thomas William Parsons

*E*very contradiction of our will, every little ailment, every petty disappointment, will become a blessing if we take it patiently. So, walking on earth, we may be in heaven. The ill tempers of others, the slights and rudenesses of the world, ill health, the daily accidents with which God has mercifully strewed our paths, instead of ruffling or disturbing our peace, may cause His peace to be shed abroad in our hearts abundantly.

Edward B. Pusey

July 18

A new commandment I give unto you, That ye love one another; as I have loved you, that ye also love one another. —John 13:34

And the Lord make you to increase and abound in love one toward another, and toward all men.
—1 Thessalonians 3:12

Let love through all my conduct shine,
An image fair, though faint, of Thine;
Thus let me His disciple prove,
Who came to manifest Thy love.

Anonymous

We should arrive at a fullness of love extending to the whole creation. We should have a desire to impart, to pour out in full and copious streams, the love and goodness we bear to all around us.

James Pierrepoint Greaves

Goodness and love mold the form into their own image and cause the joy and beauty of love to shine forth from every part of the face. When this form of love is seen, it appears ineffably beautiful and affects with delight the inmost life of the soul.

Emanuel Swedenborg

The soul within had so often lighted up her countenance with its own full happiness and joy, that something of a permanent radiance remained upon it.

Anna, or *Passages from Home Life*

July 19

The LORD is good to all: and his tender mercies are over all his works. —Psalm 145:9

For every beast of the forest is mine, and the cattle upon a thousand hills. —Psalm 50:10

Maker of earth and sea and sky,
　　Creation's sovereign Lord and King,
Who hung the starry worlds on high,
　　And formed alike the sparrow's wing;
Bless the dumb creatures of Thy care,
And listen to their voiceless prayer.

Anonymous

I believe where the love of God is truly perfected, and the true spirit of government is watchfully attended to, a tenderness towards all creatures made subject to us will be experienced. A care will be felt in us, that we do not lessen that sweetness of life in the animal creation, which the great Creator intends for them under our government. To say we love God as unseen, and at the same time exercise cruelty toward the least creature moving by His life, or by life derived from Him, is a contradiction in itself.

John Woolman

I would give nothing for that man's religion whose very dog and cat are not the better for it.

Rowland Hill

*Then I said, I have laboured in vain, I have spent my
strength for nought, and in vain.* —Isaiah 49:4

Because I spent the strength Thou gavest me
In struggle which Thou never didst ordain,
And have but dregs of life to offer Thee
    O Lord, I do repent.

                Sarah Williams

*R*emember, it is our best work that He wants,
not the dregs of our exhaustion. I think He
must prefer quality to quantity.

              George MacDonald

If the people about you are carrying on their
business or their benevolence at a pace that drains
the life out of you, resolutely take a slower pace. Be
called a straggler, make less money, accomplish less
work than they, but be what you were meant to be
and can be. You have your natural limit of power as
much as an engine—ten horsepower or twenty or a
hundred. You are fit to do certain kinds of work,
and you need a certain kind and amount of fuel, and
a certain kind of handling.

           George Spring Merriam

In your occupations, try to possess your soul in
peace. It is not a good plan to be in haste to perform
any action so that it may be over sooner. On the
contrary, you should accustom yourself to do whatever you have to do with tranquillity in order that
you may retain the possession of yourself and of settled peace.

           Madame Jeanne Guyon

July 21

For which cause we faint not; but though our outward man perish, yet the inward man is renewed day by day.
—2 Corinthians 4:16

> Let my soul beneath her load
> Faint not through the o'erwearied flesh;
> Let me hourly drink afresh
> Love and peace from Thee, my God!
>
> Christian Friedrich Richter

*I*n my attempts to promote the comfort of my family, the quiet of my spirit has been disturbed. Some of this is doubtless owing to physical weakness, but with every temptation, there is a way of escape. There is never any need to sin. Another thing I have suffered loss from is the entering into the business of the day without seeking to have my spirit quieted and directed. So many things press upon me that this is sometimes neglected. Shame on me that it should be so.

This is of great importance, to watch carefully—now I am so weak—not to overfatigue myself, because then I cannot contribute to the pleasure of others. A placid face and a gentle tone will make my family happier than anything else I can do for them. Our own will enters sadly into the performance of our duties sometimes.

Elizabeth Taber King

Whoso is wise, and will observe these things, even they
shall understand the lovingkindness of the LORD.
—Psalm 107:43

What channel needs our faith, except the eyes?
God leaves no spot of earth unglorified;
Profuse and wasteful, lovelinesses rise;
New beauties dawn before the old have died.

Trust thou thy joys in keeping of the Power
Who holds these changing shadows in His hand;
Believe and live, and know that hour by hour
Will ripple newer beauty to thy strand.

Thomas Wentworth Higginson

I wondered over again for the hundredth time
what could be the principle that, in the wildest,
most lawless, fantastically chaotic, apparently capricious work of nature, always kept it beautiful. The
beauty of holiness must be at the heart of it somehow, I thought. Because our God is so free from
stain, so loving, so unselfish, so good, so altogether
what He wants us to be, so holy, all His works declare Him in beauty. His fingers can touch nothing
except to mold it into loveliness, and even the play
of His elements is in grace and tenderness of form.

George MacDonald

Thou shalt love the Lord thy God with all thy heart, and with all thy soul, and with all thy strength, and with all thy mind. —Luke 10:27

> O God what offering shall I give
> > To Thee, the Lord of earth and skies?
> My spirit, soul, and flesh receive,
> > A holy, living sacrifice.
>
> Joachim Lange

To love God "with all our heart" is to know the spiritual passion of measureless gratitude for loving-kindness, and self-devotedness to goodness. To love Him "with all our mind" is to know the passion for truth that is the enthusiasm of science, the passion for beauty that inspires the poet and the artist, when all truth and beauty are regarded as the self-revealings of God. To love Him "with all our soul" is to know the saint's rapture of devotion and gaze of penitential awe into the face of the All-holy, the saint's abhorrence of sin and agony of desire to save a sinner's soul. And, to love Him "with all our strength" is the supreme spiritual passion that tests the rest. It shows our passion for reality, for worship in spirit and in truth, for being what we adore, for doing what we know to be God's Word. It is a test of our loyalty that exacts the living sacrifice, the whole burnt-offering that is our reasonable service, and in our coldest hours keeps steadfast to what seemed good when we were aglow.

John Hamilton Thom

July 24

Walk worthy of God, who hath called you unto his kingdom and glory. —1 Thessalonians 2:12

Surely the LORD is in this place; and I knew it not. —Genesis 28:16

Thou camest not to thy place by accident,
It is the very place God meant for thee;
And shouldst thou there small scope for action see,
Do not for this give room to discontent.

Richard Chenevix Trench

*A*ccept the place that Divine Providence has found for you, the society of your contemporaries, the connection of events.

Ralph Waldo Emerson

Adapt yourself to the things with which your lot has been cast, and love with a sincere affection the men with whom it is your portion to live. No longer be either dissatisfied with your present lot or shrink from the future.

Marcus Aurelius Antoninus

I love best to have each thing in its season, doing without it at all other times. I have never gotten over my surprise that I should have been born into the most estimable place in all the world, and in the very nick of time, too.

Henry David Thoreau

July 25

He knoweth the way that I take. —Job 23:10

Man's goings are of the LORD; how can a man then understand his own way? —Proverbs 20:24

Be quiet, why this anxious heed
About thy tangled ways?
God knows them all, He giveth speed,
And He allows delays.

E. W.

We complain of the slow, dull life we are forced to lead, of our humble sphere of action, of our low position in the scale of society, of our having no room to make ourselves known, of our wasted energies, of our years of patience. So we say that we have no Father who is directing our life. So we say that God has forgotten us. So we boldly judge what life is best for us. And so by our complaining do we lose the use and profit of the quiet years. Oh, men of little faith! Because you are not sent out yet into your labor, do you think God has ceased to remember you? Because you are forced to be outwardly inactive, do you think you may not be, in your years of quiet, about your Father's business? It is a period given to us in which to mature ourselves for the work which God will give us to do.

Stopford A. Brooke

*They that trust in the LORD shall be as mount Zion,
which cannot be removed, but abideth for ever. As the
mountains are round about Jerusalem, so the LORD is
round about his people from henceforth even for ever.*
—Psalm 125:1–2

How on a rock they stand,
Who watch His eye, and hold His guiding hand!
Not half so fixed amid her vassal hills,
Rises the holy pile that Kedron's valley fills.

John Keble

That is the way to be immovable in the midst of
troubles, as a rock amidst the waves. When
God is in the midst of a kingdom or city, He makes
it as firm as Mount Zion, which cannot be removed.
When He is in the midst of a soul, though calamities
throng about it on all hands and roar like the bil-
lows of the sea, there is a constant calm within, such
a peace as the world can neither give nor take away.
What is it but the need of lodging God in the soul,
and that in His stead the world is in men's hearts,
that makes them shake like leaves at every blast of
danger?

Robert Leighton

He that received seed into the good ground is he that heareth the word, and understandeth it; which also beareth fruit, and bringeth forth, some an hundredfold, some sixty, some thirty. —Matthew 13:23

> Then bless thy secret growth, nor catch
> At noise, but thrive unseen and dumb;
> Keep clean, bear fruit, earn life, and watch
> Till the white-wingèd reapers come.
>
> Henry Vaughan

He does not need to transplant us into a different field. Right where we are, with just the circumstances that surround us, He makes His sun to shine and His dew to fall upon us. He transforms the very things that were before our greatest hindrances into the chiefest and most blessed means of our growth. No difficulties in your case can baffle Him. No dwarfing of your growth in years that are past, no apparent dryness of your inward springs of life, no crookedness or deformity in any of your past development, can in the least mar the perfect work that He will accomplish if you will only put yourselves absolutely into His hands and let Him have His own way with you.

Hannah Whitall Smith

But I would not have you to be ignorant, brethren, concerning them which are asleep, that ye sorrow not, even as others which have no hope. —1 Thessalonians 4:13

Yet Love will dream and Faith will trust
   (Since He who knows our need is just),
That somehow, somewhere, meet we must.
   Alas for him who never sees
   The stars shine through his cypress trees;
Who hath not learned in hours of faith,
   The truth to flesh and sense unknown,
That life is ever Lord of Death,
   And Love can never lose its own.
John Greenleaf Whittier

*W*hile we poor wayfarers still toil, with hot and bleeding feet, along the highway and the dust of life, our companions have but mounted the divergent path to explore the more sacred streams and visit the heavenly vales and wander amid the everlasting alps of God's upper province of creation. And so we keep up the courage of our hearts and refresh ourselves with the memories of love. We travel forward in the ways of duty, with less weary step, feeling always for the hand of God and listening for the domestic voices of the immortals whose happy welcome waits us. Death, in short, under the Christian aspect, is but God's method of colonization, the transition from this mother country of our race to the fairer and newer world of our emigration.
James Martineau

But this I say, brethren, the time is short.
—1 Corinthians 7:29

I sometimes feel the thread of life is slender,
And soon with me the labor will be wrought;
Then grows my heart to other hearts more tender.
The time is short.

Dinah Maria Craik

Oh, my dear friends, you who are letting miserable misunderstandings run on from year to year, meaning to clear them up some day, if you only could know and see and feel, all of a sudden, that *"the time is short."* You who are keeping wretched quarrels alive because you cannot quite make up your mind that now is the day to sacrifice your pride and kill them, if only you could know this as well. You who are passing men sullenly upon the street, not speaking to them out of some silly spite, and yet knowing that it would fill you with shame and remorse if you heard that one of those men were dead tomorrow morning, you need to know this. You who are letting your neighbor starve, until you hear that he is dying of starvation; or letting your friend's heart ache for a word of appreciation or sympathy, which you mean to give him some day, if you only could know! How it would break the spell! How you would go instantly and do the thing that you might never have another chance to do.

Phillips Brooks

Remember not the sins of my youth, nor my transgressions: according to thy mercy remember thou me for thy goodness' sake, O LORD. —Psalm 25:7

When on my aching, burdened heart
My sins lie heavily,
My pardon speak, new peace impart,
In love remember me.

Thomas Haweis

We need to know that our sins are forgiven. And how will we know this? By feeling that we have peace with God. By feeling that we are able so to trust in the divine compassion and infinite tenderness of our Father, as to arise and go to Him whenever we commit sin and say at once to Him, "Father, I have sinned; forgive me." To know that we are forgiven, it is only necessary to look at our Father's love until it sinks into our heart. It is only necessary to open our soul to Him until He will pour His love into it. It is only necessary to wait on Him until we find peace, until our conscience no longer torments us, until the weight of responsibility ceases to be an oppressive burden to us, until we can feel that our sins, great as they are, cannot keep us away from our heavenly Father.

James Freeman Clarke

*I have blotted out, as a thick cloud, thy transgressions,
and, as a cloud, thy sins: return unto me; for I have
redeemed thee. —Isaiah 44:22*

*He will turn again, he will have compassion upon us;
he will subdue our iniquities; and thou wilt cast all
their sins into the depths of the sea. —Micah 7:19*

If my shut eyes should dare their lids to part,
I know how they must quail beneath the blaze
Of Thy Love's greatness. No; I dare not raise
One prayer, to look aloft, lest it should gaze
On such forgiveness as would break my heart.
                                    Henry Septimus Sutton

O Lord God, gracious and merciful, give us, I entreat You, a humble trust in Your mercy, and
do not allow our hearts to fail us. Though our sins
be seven, though our sins be seventy times seven,
though our sins be more in number than the hairs
of our heads, give us grace in loving penitence to
cast ourselves down into the depth of Your compassion. Let us fall into the hand of the Lord. Amen.
                                    Christina G. Rossetti

*Be not hasty in thy spirit to be angry: for anger resteth
in the bosom of fools.* —Ecclesiastes 7:9

Let not the sun go down upon your wrath.
—Ephesians 4:26

Quench thou the fires of hate and strife,
The wasting fever of the heart;
From perils guard our feeble life,
And to our souls Thy peace impart.
Cardinal John Henry Newman,
Translated from Latin

*W*hen you are offended or annoyed by others,
do not allow your thoughts to dwell on them
or on anything relating to them. For example, don't
think that they ought not to have treated you so,
being who they are, or whom they think themselves
to be, or the like. All this is fuel and kindling of
wrath, anger, and hatred.

Lorenzo Scupoli

Struggle diligently against your impatience,
and strive to be amiable and gentle, in season and
out of season towards everyone, however much they
may vex and annoy you. Be sure, then, that God will
bless your efforts.

Francis de Sales

August 2

Behold, God is my salvation; I will trust, and not be afraid: for the LORD JEHOVAH is my strength and my song; he also is become my salvation. —Isaiah 12:2

Why are ye so fearful? how is it that ye have no faith?
—Mark 4:40

> Still heavy is thy heart?
> Still sink thy spirits down?
> Cast off the weight, let fear depart,
> And every care be gone.
>
> Paul Gerhardt

Go on in all simplicity. Do not be so anxious to obtain a quiet mind, and it will be all the quieter. Do not examine so closely the progress of your soul. Do not crave so much to be perfect, but let your spiritual life be formed by your duties and by the actions that are called forth by circumstances. Do not take too much thought for tomorrow. God, who has led you safely on so far, will lead you on to the end. Be altogether at rest in the loving holy confidence that you ought to have in His heavenly providence.

Francis de Sales

August 3

Thou hast made him exceeding glad with thy
countenance. —Psalm 21:6

My heart for gladness springs,
   It cannot more be sad,
For very joy it laughs and sings,
   Sees nought but sunshine glad.

Paul Gerhardt

A new day rose upon me. It was as if another sun had risen into the sky. The heavens were indescribably brighter, and the earth fairer, and that day has gone on brightening to the present hour. I have known the other joys of life, I suppose, as much as most men. I have known art and beauty, music and gladness. I have known friendship and love and family ties, but it is certain that until we see God in the world—God in the bright and boundless universe—we never know the highest joy. It is far more than if one were translated to a world a thousand times fairer than this, for that supreme and central Light of Infinite Love and Wisdom, shining over this world and all worlds, alone can show us how noble and beautiful, how fair and glorious they are.

Orville Dewey

When I look like this into the blue sky, it seems so deep, so peaceful, so full of a mysterious tenderness, that I could lie for centuries and wait for the dawning of the face of God out of the awe-inspiring loving-kindness.

George MacDonald

August 4

He satisfieth the longing soul, and filleth the hungry
soul with goodness. —Psalm 107:9

That ye might be filled with all the fulness of God.
—Ephesians 3:19

Enough that He who made can fill the soul
    Here and hereafter till its deeps o'erflow;
Enough that love and tenderness control
    Our fate where'er in joy or doubt we go.

                           Anonymous

O God, the Life of the faithful, the Bliss of the righteous, mercifully receive the prayers of Your suppliants, so that the souls that thirst for Your promises may evermore be filled from Your abundance. Amen.

Gelasian Sacramentary, A.D. 490

God makes every common thing serve, if you will, to enlarge that capacity of bliss in His love. There is no prayer that does not enlarge the whole soul for the endless capacity of the love of God. There is no act of faithfulness in your calling, no self-denying or kind word or deed done out of love for Himself, that does not make one more able to love God. Not a weariness or painfulness endured patiently, not a duty performed, not a temptation resisted, but that it enlarges the soul's ability to love God.

                         Edward B. Pusey

August 5

Thanks be unto God for his unspeakable gift.
—2 Corinthians 9:15

O Giver of each perfect gift!
This day our daily bread supply;
While from the Spirit's tranquil depths
We drink unfailing draughts of joy.

Lyra Catholica

*T*he best way for a man rightly to enjoy himself is to maintain a universal, ready, and cheerful compliance with the divine and uncreated will in all things. He should know that nothing can issue and flow forth from the fountain of goodness but that which is good. Therefore, a good man is never offended with any piece of divine dispensation. And he never has any reluctance against that will, which dictates and determines all things by an eternal rule of goodness. He knows that there is an unbounded and almighty Love that without any disdain or envy freely communicates itself to everything God made, that always enfolds in His everlasting arms those who are made partakers of His own image. Almighty Love is perpetually nourishing and cherishing them with the fresh and vital influences of His grace.

Dr. John Smith

August 6

Bless the LORD, O my soul, and forget not all his benefits. —Psalm 103:2

Wiser it were to welcome and make ours
Whate'er of good, though small, the Present brings,
Kind greetings, sunshine, song of birds, and flowers,
With a child's pure delight in little things.

Richard Chenevix Trench

*I*nto all our lives, in many simple, familiar, homely ways, God infuses this element of joy from the surprises of life, which unexpectedly brighten our days and fill our eyes with light. He drops this added sweetness into His children's cup and makes it to run over. The success we were not counting on, the blessing we were not trying after, the strain of music in the midst of drudgery, the beautiful morning picture or sunset glory thrown in as we pass to or from our daily business, the unsought word of encouragement or expression of sympathy, the sentence that meant for us more than the writer or speaker thought: these and a hundred others that everyone's experience can supply are instances of what I mean. You may call it accident or chance, for it often is. You may call it human goodness, for it often is. But always, always call it God's love, for that is always in it. These are the overflowing riches of His grace; these are His free gifts.

Samuel Longfellow

August 7

If thou canst believe, all things are possible to him that believeth. —Mark 9:23

Nothing shall be impossible unto you. —Matthew 17:20

> So nigh is grandeur to our dust,
> So near is God to man,
> When Duty whispers low, *Thou must,*
> The youth replies, *I can.*
>
> Ralph Waldo Emerson

*K*now that "impossible," where truth and mercy and the everlasting voice of nature order, has no place in the brave man's dictionary. When all men have said, "Impossible," and tumbled noisily elsewhere, and you alone are left, then first your time and possibility have come. It is for you now. Do that, and ask no man's counsel but your own only and God's. Brother, you have possibility in you for much: the possibility of writing on the eternal skies the record of a heroic life.

Thomas Carlyle

In the moral world there is nothing impossible, if we bring a thorough will to it. Man can do everything with himself, but he must not attempt to do too much with others.

Karl Wilhelm von Humboldt

August 8

Stand fast therefore in the liberty wherewith Christ hath made us free, and be not entangled again with the yoke of bondage. —Galatians 5:1

I believed, and therefore have I spoken.
—2 Corinthians 4:13

They are slaves who fear to speak
For the fallen and the weak;
They are slaves who will not choose
Hatred, scoffing, and abuse,
Rather than in silence shrink
From the truth they needs must think;
They are slaves who dare not be
In the right with two or three.

James Russell Lowell

The real corrupters of society may not be the corrupt but those who have held back the righteous leaven. It may be the salt that has lost its savor or the innocent who do not have even the moral courage to show what they think of the effrontery of impurity. It could also be the serious who yet timidly succumb before some loud-voiced scoffer, or even the heart trembling all over with religious sensibilities that yet allows itself through false shame to be beaten down into outward and practical acquiescence by some rude and worldly nature.

John Hamilton Thom

August 9

*And he said, The things which are impossible with men
are possible with God.* —Luke 18:27

*Unless the LORD had been my help, my soul had almost
dwelt in silence.* —Psalm 94:17

When obstacles and trials seem
Like prison-walls to be,
I do the little I can do,
And leave the rest to Thee.
Frederick William Faber

*T*he mind never puts forth greater power over
itself than when, in great trials, it yields up
calmly its desires, affections, and interests to God.
There are seasons when to be still demands im-
measurably higher strength than to act. Composure
is often the highest result of power. Do you think it
demands no power to calm the stormy elements of
passion, to moderate the vehemence of desire, to
throw off the load of dejection, to suppress every
repining thought when the dearest hopes are withered, and to turn the wounded spirit from dangerous reveries and wasting grief to the quiet discharge
of ordinary duties? Is there no power put forth,
when a man, stripped of his property, of the fruits of
a life's labors, quells discontent and gloomy forebodings, and serenely and patiently returns to the
tasks that Providence assigns?

William Ellery Channing

*The cup which my Father hath given me, shall I not
drink it?* —John 18:11

Every sorrow, every smart,
That the Eternal Father's heart
Hath appointed me of yore,
Or hath yet for me in store,
As my life flows on, I'll take
Calmly, gladly, for his sake,
No more faithless murmurs make.

Paul Gerhardt

*T*he very least and the very greatest sorrows
that God ever allows to befall you, proceed
from the depths of His unspeakable love. Such great
love is better for you than the highest and best gifts
that He has given you, or ever could give you, if you
could but see it in this light. So that if your little
finger only aches, if you are cold, if you are hungry
or thirsty, if others irritate you by their words or
deeds, or whatever happens to you that causes you
distress or pain, it will all help to fit you for a noble
and blessed state.

John Tauler

August 11

The LORD thy God shall bless thee in all thy works, and in all that thou puttest thine hand unto.
—Deuteronomy 15:10

My place of lowly service, too,
    Beneath Thy sheltering wings I see;
For all the work I have to do
    Is done through sheltering rest in Thee.

Anna Laetitia Waring

I think I find most help in trying to look on all interruptions and hindrances to the work that I have planned out for myself as discipline and as trials sent by God to help me from getting too caught up in my work. Then I can feel that perhaps my true work, my work for God, consists in doing some trifling haphazard thing that has been thrown into my day. It is not a waste of time, as one is tempted to think. It is the most important part of the work of the day, the part one can best offer to God. After such a hindrance, do not rush after the planned work. Trust that the time to finish it will be given sometime, and keep a quiet heart about it.

Annie Keary

August 12

Master, what shall I do to inherit eternal life?
—Luke 10:25

Whatsoever thy hand findeth to do, do it with thy might. —Ecclesiastes 9:10

"What shall I do to gain eternal life?"
    "Discharge aright
The simple dues with which each day is rife,
    Yea, with thy might."

                Friedrich von Schiller

A man is relieved and happy when he has put his heart into his work and done his best, but what he has said or done otherwise will give him no peace.

                Ralph Waldo Emerson

Be diligent, after your power, to do deeds of love. Think nothing too little, nothing too low, to do lovingly for the sake of God. Bear with infirmities, ungentle tempers, contradictions. Visit, if you may, the sick. Relieve the poor. Forego yourself and your own ways for love, and He whom in them you love, to whom in them you minister, will own your love and will pour His own love into you.

                Edward B. Pusey

In your patience possess ye your souls. —Luke 21:19

> What though thy way be dark, and earth
> With ceaseless care do cark, till mirth
>   To thee no sweet strain singeth;
> Still hide thy life above, and still
> Believe that God is love; fulfill
>   Whatever lot He bringeth.
>
> Albert Eubule Evans

*T*he soul loses command of itself when it is impatient. Whereas, when it submits without a murmur, it possesses itself in peace, and possesses God. To be impatient is to desire what we do not have, or not to desire what we have. When we acquiesce in a trial, it is no longer such. Why make a real calamity of it by resistance? Peace does not dwell in outward things but within the soul. We may preserve it in the midst of the bitterest pain, if our will remains firm and submissive. Peace in this life springs from acquiescence even in disagreeable things, not in an exemption from bearing them.

Fénelon

The chief pang of most trials is not so much the actual suffering itself, as our own spirit of resistance to it.

Jean Nicolas Grou

August 14

I will lift up mine eyes unto the hills, from whence cometh my help. —Psalm 121:1

My grace is sufficient for thee. —2 Corinthians 12:9

> I look to Thee in every need,
> And never look in vain;
> I feel Thy touch, Eternal Love,
> And all is well again:
> The thought of Thee is mightier far
> Than sin and pain and sorrow are.
>
> Samuel Longfellow

*H*ow can you live sweetly amid the annoying things, the irritating things, the multitude of little worries and frets, which lie all along your way and which you cannot evade? You cannot at present change your surroundings. Whatever kind of life you are to live must be lived amid precisely the experiences in which you are now moving. Here you must win your victories or suffer your defeats. No restlessness or discontent can change your lot. Others may have other circumstances surrounding them, but here are yours. You had better make up your mind to accept what you cannot alter. You can live a beautiful life in the midst of your present circumstances.

J. R. Miller

Strive to realize a state of inward happiness, independent of circumstances.

James Pierrepoint Greaves

*God hath not given us the spirit of fear; but of power,
and of love, and of a sound mind.* —2 Timothy 1:7

We cast behind fear, sin, and death;
   With Thee we seek the things above;
Our inmost souls Thy spirit breathe,
   Of power, of calmness, and of love.
Hymns of the Spirit

I must conclude with a more delightful subject:
my most dear and blessed sister. I never saw a
more perfect instance of the spirit of power and of
love, and of a sound mind. She had an intense love,
almost to the annihilation of selfishness. Hers was a
daily martyrdom for twenty years, during which she
adhered to her early-formed resolution of never
talking about herself. She was thoughtful about the
very pins and ribbons of my wife's dress or about
the making of a doll's cap for a child. But of herself,
save only as regarded her ripening in all goodness,
she was wholly thoughtless, enjoying everything
lovely, graceful, beautiful, high-minded, whether in
God's works or man's, with the keenest relish. She
inherited the earth to the very fullness of the
promise, though never leaving her dwelling or
changing her posture. She was saved, through the
very valley of the shadow of death, from all fear or
impatience, or from every cloud of impaired reason,
which might mar the beauty of Christ's spirit's glorious work.

Thomas Arnold

Whatsoever a man soweth, that shall he also reap.
—Galatians 6:7

> The life above, when this is past,
>   Is the ripe fruit of life below.
>
> Sow love, and taste its fruitage pure;
>   Sow peace, and reap its harvest bright;
> Sow sunbeams on the rock and moor,
>   And find a harvest-home of light.
>
>   Horatius Bonar

*T*he dispositions, affections, and inclinations of soul that will emerge hereafter in perfection, must be trained and nurtured in us throughout the whole course of this earthly life. When will we bear in mind this plain truth: that the future perfection of the saints is not a translation from one state or disposition of soul into another, diverse from the former? Rather, it is the carrying out, and, as it were, the blossom and the fruitage of one and the same principle of spiritual life. This principle, through our whole career on earth, has been growing with an even strength, putting itself forth in the beginnings and promise of perfection, reaching upward with steadfast aspirations after perfect holiness.

                               Cardinal Henry Edward Manning

*O turn unto me, and have mercy upon me; give thy
strength unto thy servant, and save the son of thine
handmaid.* —Psalm 86:16

Thou art my King
My King henceforth alone;
And I, Thy servant, Lord, am all Thine own.
Give me Thy strength; oh! let Thy dwelling be
In this poor heart that pants, my Lord, for Thee!
Gerhard Tersteegen

*W*hen it is the one, ruling, never-ceasing desire
of our hearts that God may be the beginning
and end, the reason and motive, the rule and measure, of our doing or not doing from morning to
night, then we are offered up to the eternal Spirit.
Everywhere, whether speaking or silent, whether
inwardly or outwardly employed, we have our life in
Him and from Him. We are united to Him by that
Spirit of Prayer which is the comfort, the support,
the strength and security of the soul, traveling by
the help of God through the vanity of time into the
riches of eternity. Let us have no thought or care
except how to be wholly His devoted instruments,
everywhere, and in everything, His adoring, joyful,
and thankful servants.

William Law

Beloved, if our heart condemn us not, then have we con-fidence toward God. —1 John 3:21

O Lord, how happy is the time
When in Thy love I rest:
When from my weariness I climb
E'en to Thy tender breast.
The night of sorrow endeth there,
Thy rays outshine the sun;
And in Thy pardon and Thy care
The heaven of heavens is won.

Wolfgang Christoph Dessler

*N*othing does so much establish the mind amidst the rolling and turbulence of present things, as both a look above them and a look beyond them: above them to the good and steady Hand by which they are ruled and beyond them to the sweet and beautiful end to which, by that Hand, they will be brought. Study pure and holy walking, if you would have your confidence firm, and have boldness and joy in God. You will find that a little sin will shake your trust and disturb your peace more than the greatest sufferings. Yes, in those sufferings, your assurance and joy in God will grow and abound most if sin is kept out. However much sin gets in, that much peace will go out.

Robert Leighton

Teach me thy way, O LORD, and lead me in a plain path. —Psalm 27:11

Lead, kindly Light, amid the encircling gloom,
    Lead Thou me on;
The night is dark, and I am far from home,
    Lead Thou me on.
Keep Thou my feet; I do not ask to see
The distant scene; one step enough for me.
        Cardinal John Henry Newman

*G*od only is holy. He alone knows how to lead His children in the paths of holiness. He knows every aspect of your soul, every thought of your heart, every secret of your character, its difficulties and hindrances. He knows how to mold you to His will and lead you onward to perfect sanctification. He knows exactly how each event, each trial, each temptation will affect you, and He disposes all things accordingly. The consequences of this belief, if fully grasped, will influence your whole life. You will seek to give yourself up to God more and more unreservedly, asking nothing, refusing nothing, wishing nothing, but what He wills. You will not seek to bring things about for yourself, taking all He sends joyfully, and believing the "one step" set before you to be enough for you. You will be satisfied that even though there are clouds around, and your way seems dark, He is directing all, and that what seems a hindrance will prove a blessing, since He wills it.

Jean Nicolas Grou

Wait on the LORD: be of good courage, and he shall strengthen thine heart: wait, I say, on the LORD.
—Psalm 27:14

He giveth power to the faint; and to them that have no might he increaseth strength. —Isaiah 40:29

Leaning on Him, make with reverent meekness
     His own thy will,
And with strength from Him shall thy utter weakness
     Life's task fulfill.

                John Greenleaf Whittier

*I*f we feel at times disheartened and discouraged, a confiding thought, a simple movement of heart towards God will renew our powers. Whatever He may demand of us, He will give us, at the moment, the strength and the courage that we need.

                Fénelon

We require a certain firmness in all circumstances of life, even the happiest, and perhaps contradictions come in order to prove and exercise this. And, if we can only determine so to use them, the very effort brings back tranquillity to the soul, which always enjoys having exercised its strength in conformity to duty.

           Karl Wilhelm von Humboldt

We then that are strong ought to bear the infirmities of the weak, and not to please ourselves. —Romans 15:1

The Lord GOD hath given me the tongue of the learned, that I should know how to speak a word in season to him that is weary. —Isaiah 50:4

> If there be some weaker one,
> Give me strength to help him on;
> If a blinder soul there be,
> Let me guide him nearer Thee.
>
> John Greenleaf Whittier

*A*sk Him to increase your powers of sympathy, to give you more quickness and depth of sympathy in little things as well as great. Opportunities of doing a kindness are often lost from mere lack of thought. Half a dozen lines of kindness may bring sunshine into the whole day of some sick person. Think of the pleasure you might give to someone who is much shut up, and who has fewer pleasures than you have, by sharing with him or her some little comfort or enjoyment that you have learned to look upon as a necessity of life: the pleasant drive, the new book, flowers from the country, etc. Try to put yourself in another's place. Ask "What should I like myself if I were overworked or sick or lonely?" Cultivate the habit of sympathy.

G. H. Wilkinson

August 22

*I beseech you therefore, brethren, by the mercies of God,
that ye present your bodies a living sacrifice, holy, acceptable unto God, which is your reasonable service.*
—Romans 12:1

Thou hast my flesh, Thy hallowed shrine,
  Devoted solely to Thy will;
Here let Thy light forever shine,
  This house still let Thy presence fill;
O Source of Life, live, dwell, and move
In me, till all my life be love!

Joachim Lange

*I*s it not a comfort to those of us who feel we do
not have the mental or spiritual power that others have, to notice that the living sacrifice men-
tioned in Romans 12:1 is our *"bodies"*? Of course,
that includes the mental power, but does it not also
include the loving, sympathizing glance, the kind,
encouraging word, the ready errand for another, the
work of our hands? These are opportunities all of
which come more often in the day than the mental
power we are often tempted to envy. May we be enabled to offer willingly that which we have.

Anonymous

August 23

Seekest thou great things for thyself? seek them not.
—Jeremiah 45:5

> I would not have the restless will
> That hurries to and fro,
> Seeking for some great thing to do,
> Or secret thing to know;
> I would be treated as a child,
> And guided where I go.
> Anna Laetitia Waring

Oh! Be little, be little, and then you will be content with little. And if you feel, now and then, a check or a secret smiting, in that is the Father's love. Do not be overwise or overeager in your own willing, running, and desiring, and you may feel it so. By degrees you will come to the knowledge of your Guide, who will lead you, step by step, in the path of life and teach you to follow. Be still, and wait for light and strength.

Isaac Penington

Sink into the sweet and blessed littleness, where you live by grace alone. Contemplate with delight the holiness and goodness in God, which you do not find in yourself. How lovely it is to be nothing when God is all!

Gerhard Tersteegen

And that which fell among thorns are they, which,
when they have heard, go forth, and are choked with
cares and riches and pleasures of this life, and bring no
fruit to perfection. —Luke 8:14

Preserve me from my calling's snare,
And hide my simple heart above,
Above the thorns of choking care,
The gilded baits of worldly love.

Charles Wesley

*A*nything allowed in the heart that is contrary to the will of God, whether it seems ever so insignificant, or is ever so deeply hidden, will cause us to fall before our enemies. Any root of bitterness cherished towards another, any self-seeking, any harsh judgments indulged in, any slackness in obeying the voice of the Lord, any doubtful habits or surroundings—any one of these things will effectually cripple and paralyze our spiritual life. I believe our blessed Guide, the indwelling Holy Spirit, is always secretly exposing these things to us by continual little twinges and pangs of conscience, so that we are left without excuse.

Hannah Whitall Smith

August 25

See that ye refuse not him that speaketh.
—Hebrews 12:25

> From the world of sin and noise
>   And hurry I withdraw;
> For the small and inward voice
>   I wait with humble awe;
> Silent am I now and still,
>   Dare not in Thy presence move;
> To my waiting soul reveal
>   The secret of Thy love.
>
> Charles Wesley

When therefore the smallest instinct or desire of your heart calls you towards God and a newness of life, give it time and leave to speak, and take care that you do not refuse Him who speaks. Be retired, silent, submissive, and humbly attentive to this new risen light within you.

William Law

It is hardly to be wondered at that he should lose the finer consciousness of higher powers and deeper feelings. It was not from any behavior in itself wrong, but from the hurry, noise, and tumult in the streets of life, that, penetrating too deep into the house of life, dazed and stupefied the silent and lonely watcher in the distant chamber of conscience. He had no time to think or feel.

George MacDonald

Be silent, O all flesh, before the LORD. —Zechariah 2:13

> Be earth, with all her scenes, withdrawn;
> Let noise and vanity be gone:
> In secret silence of the mind,
> My heaven, and there my God, I find.
>
> Isaac Watts

*I*t is only with the pious affection of the will that we can be spiritually attentive to God. As long as the noisy restlessness of the thoughts goes on, the gentle and holy desires of the new nature are overpowered and inactive.

James Pierrepoint Greaves

There is hardly ever a complete silence in our soul. God is whispering to us almost incessantly. Whenever the sounds of the world die out in the soul, or sink low, then we hear these whisperings of God. He is always whispering to us, only we do not always hear because of the noise, hurry, and distraction that life causes as it rushes on.

Frederick William Faber

The prayer of faith is a sincere, sweet, and quiet view of divine, eternal truth. The soul rests quietly, perceiving and loving God, sweetly rejecting all the imaginations that present themselves, calming the mind in the divine presence, and fixing it only on God.

Miguel Molinos

Being confident of this very thing, that he which hath begun a good work in you will perform it.
—Philippians 1:6

He that endureth to the end shall be saved.
—Matthew 10:22

Fill with inviolable peace;
   Stablish and keep my settled heart;
In Thee may all my wanderings cease,
   From Thee no more may I depart:
Thy utmost goodness called to prove,
Loved with an everlasting love!

Charles Wesley

*I*f any sincere Christian were to cast himself with his whole will upon the Divine Presence that dwells within him, he would be kept safe until the end. What is it that makes us unable to persevere? Is it need of strength? By no means. We have with us the strength of the Holy Spirit. When did we ever set ourselves sincerely to any work according to the will of God and fail for need of strength? It was not that strength failed the will, but that the will failed first. If we could but embrace the divine will with the whole of our love, cleaving to it and holding fast by it, we should be borne along, as upon the *"river of water of life"* (Rev. 22:1). We open only certain chambers of our will to the influence of the divine will. We are afraid of being wholly absorbed into it. And yet, if we would have peace, we must be altogether united with Him.

Cardinal Henry Edward Manning

August 28

*They that know thy name will put their trust in thee: for
thou, LORD, hast not forsaken them that seek thee.*
                    —Psalm 9:10

Yea, the LORD shall give that which is good.
                    —Psalm 85:12

In Thee I place my trust,
    On Thee I calmly rest;
I know Thee good, I know Thee just,
    And count Thy choice the best.

                    Henry Francis Lyte

*T*he souls who desire to be richer in duty in
some new position are precisely those who borrow no excuses from the old position. They see it as
full of privileges, plenteous in occasions of good, frequent in divine appeals, and they chide their graceless and unloving temper for not seeing more of
such things. Those who are discontent and quarrel
with their tools instead of with their skills are
wretched and barren, and, by criticizing Providence,
they manage to keep up complacency with self. How
gentle we would be, if we were not provoked. How
pious we would be, if we were not busy.

The sick can be patient, despite not being in
health. The obscure can do great things, even if
these things are not conspicuous!

                    James Martineau

August 29

Am I my brother's keeper? —Genesis 4:9

Because I held upon my selfish road,
And left my brother wounded by the way,
And called ambition duty, and pressed on,
                  O Lord, I do repent.
                             Sarah Williams

*H*ow many are the sufferers who have fallen among misfortunes along the wayside of life! "By chance," we come that way. Chance, accident, or Providence has thrown them in our way. We see them from a distance, like the priest, or we come upon them suddenly, like the Levite. Our business, our pleasure, is interrupted by the sight, is troubled by the delay. What are our feelings, our actions towards them? Who is your neighbor? It is the sufferer, wherever, whoever, whatever he is. Wherever you hear the cry of distress, wherever you see anyone brought across your path by the chances and changes of life—that is, by the providence of God—whom it is in your power to help, he, whether he is a stranger or an enemy, he is your neighbor.

                        Arthur Penrhyn Stanley

Walk worthy of the vocation wherewith ye are called, with all lowliness and meekness, with longsuffering, forbearing one another in love. —Ephesians 4:1–2

Help us, O Lord, with patient love to bear
    Each other's faults, to suffer with true meekness;
Help us each other's joys and griefs to share,
    But let us turn to Thee alone in weakness.

Anonymous

*Y*ou should make a special point of asking God every morning to give you, before all else, that true spirit of meekness which He would have His children possess. You must also make a firm resolution to practice this virtue yourself, especially in your dealings with those persons to whom you chiefly owe it. You must make it your main objective to conquer yourself in this matter. Call it to mind a hundred times during the day, commending your efforts to God. It seems to me that no more than this is needed in order to subject your soul entirely to His will, and then you will become more gentle day by day, trusting wholly in His goodness. You will be very happy, my dearest child, if you can do this, for God will dwell in your heart, and where He reigns all is peace. But if you should fail, and commit some of your old faults, do not be disheartened, but rise up and go on again as though you had not fallen.

Francis de Sales

*Be of good courage, and he shall strengthen your heart,
all ye that hope in the LORD.* —Psalm 31:24

> Go, bury thy sorrow,
>   The world hath its share;
> Go, bury it deeply,
>   Go, hide it with care.
> Go, bury thy sorrow,
>   Let others be blest;
> Go, give them the sunshine,
>   And tell God the rest.

Anonymous

Our veiled and terrible guest, trouble, brings for us, if we will accept it, the boon of fortitude, patience, self-control, wisdom, sympathy, faith. If we reject it, then we find in our hands the other gifts: cowardice, weakness, isolation, despair. If your trouble seems to have in it no other possibility of good, at least set yourself to bear it heartily. Let none of its weight come on other shoulders. Try to carry it so that no one will even see it. Though your heart is sad within, let cheer go out from you to others. Meet them with a kindly presence, considerate words, helpful acts.

George Spring Merriam

September 1

Let them that suffer according to the will of God commit the keeping of their souls to him in well doing, as unto a faithful Creator. —1 Peter 4:19

The Lord is very pitiful, and of tender mercy.
—James 5:11

On Thy compassion I repose
In weakness and distress:
I will not ask for greater ease,
Lest I should love Thee less.
Oh, 't is a blessed thing for me
To need Thy tenderness.

Anna Laetitia Waring

Oh, do not look at your pain or sorrow, how great it is. But look from them, look off them, look beyond them, to the Deliverer, whose power is over them, and whose loving, wise, and tender spirit is able to do you good by them. The Lord will lead you, day by day, in the right way and keep your mind stayed upon Him, in whatever befalls you, so that the belief of His love and hope in His mercy, when you are at the lowest ebb, may keep your head up above the waves.

Isaac Penington

Blessed are the peacemakers: for they shall be called the children of God. —Matthew 5:9

Grant us Thy peace, down from Thy presence falling,
    As on the thirsty earth cool night-dews sweet;
Grant us Thy peace, to Thy pure paths recalling,
    From devious ways, our worn and wandering feet.
                        Eliza Scudder

O God, You who are peace everlasting, who have taught us that the peacemakers are Your children, and whose chosen reward is the gift of peace, pour Your sweet peace into our souls, so that everything discordant may utterly vanish, and all that makes for peace be sweet to us forever. Amen.

Gelasian Sacramentary, A.D. 492

Have you ever thought seriously of the meaning of that blessing given to the peacemakers? People are always expecting to get peace in heaven, but you know whatever peace they get there will be ready-made. They will be blessed only for the peace they make here on earth: not for taking arms against others, but for building nests amid the sea of troubles, as the halcyons do. Do you think this is difficult enough? Perhaps so, but I do not see that any of us try. We complain of the lack of many things: we lack votes, we lack liberty, we lack amusement, we lack money. Which of us feels or knows that he lacks peace?

                        John Ruskin

The eyes of all wait upon thee; and thou givest them their meat in due season. —Psalm 145:15

What time I am afraid, I will trust in thee.
—Psalm 56:3

Late on me, weeping, did this whisper fall:
"Dear child, there is no need to weep at all!
Why go about to grieve and to despair?
Why weep now through thy Future's eyes, and bear
In vain today tomorrow's load of care?"

Henry Septimus Sutton

*T*he crosses of the present moment always bring their own special grace and consequent comfort with them. We see the hand of God in them when it is laid upon us. But the crosses of anxious foreboding are seen out of the dispensation of God. We see them without grace to bear them. We see them indeed through a faithless spirit that banishes grace. So, everything in them is bitter and unendurable. All seems dark and helpless. Let us throw self aside. No more self-interest, and then God's will, unfolding every moment in everything, will console us also every moment for all that He will do around us or within us for our discipline.

Fénelon

His delight is in the law of the LORD; and in his law doth he meditate day and night. And he shall be like a tree planted by the rivers of water, that bringeth forth his fruit in his season; his leaf also shall not wither; and whatsoever he doeth shall prosper. —Psalm 1:2–3

> The wind that blows can never kill
> The tree God plants;
> It bloweth east; it bloweth west;
> The tender leaves have little rest,
> But any wind that blows is best.
> The tree God plants
> Strikes deeper root, grows higher still,
> Spreads wider boughs, for God's good-will
> Meets all its wants.

Lillie E. Barr

It is a fatal mistake to suppose that we cannot be holy except in the circumstances of life that will suit ourselves. It is one of the first principles of holiness to leave our times and our places, our going out and our coming in, our wasted and our goodly heritages entirely with the Lord. Here, O Lord, have You placed us, and we will glorify You here!

Thomas Cogswell Upham

It is not by change of circumstances, but by fitting our spirits to the circumstances in which God has placed us, that we can be reconciled to life and duty.

Frederick William Robertson

September 5

> Being perplexed I say,
>   Lord, make it right!
> Night is as day to Thee,
>   Darkness is light.
> I am afraid to touch
> Things that involve so much;
>   My trembling hand may shake,
>   My skill-less hand may break:
>   Thine can make no mistake.
>   Anna B. Warner

The many troubles in your household will be to your edification if you strive to bear them all in gentleness, patience, and kindness. Keep this ever before you, and remember constantly that God's loving eyes are upon you amid all these little worries and vexations, watching whether you take them as He would desire. Offer up all such occasions to Him, and if sometimes you are vexed, and give way to impatience, do not be discouraged, but make haste to regain your lost composure.

Francis de Sales

And he said to them all, If any man will come after me, let him deny himself, and take up his cross daily, and follow me. —Luke 9:23

There lies thy cross; beneath it meekly bow;
　　It fits thy stature now;
Who scornful pass it with averted eye,
　　'T will crush them by and by.

John Keble

*T*o take up the cross of Christ is no great action done once for all. It consists in the continual practice of small duties that are distasteful to us.

Cardinal John Henry Newman

On one occasion an intimate friend of his was fretting somewhat at not being able to put a cross on the grave of a relation because the rest of the family disliked it. "Don't you see," he said to her, "that by giving up your own way, you will be virtually putting a cross on the grave? You'll have it in its effect. The one is but a stone cross, the other is a true spiritual cross."

Life of James Hinton

I would have you, one by one, ask yourselves, In what way do I take up the cross daily?

Edward B. Pusey

Every morning, receive your own special cross from the hands of your heavenly Father.

Lorenzo Scupoli

September 7

*Pure religion and undefiled before God and the Father
is this, To visit the fatherless and widows in their affliction, and to keep himself unspotted from the world.*
—James 1:27

> Not to ease and aimless quiet
>   Does that inward answer tend,
> But to works of love and duty
>   As our being's end.
>
> John Greenleaf Whittier

*I*t is surprising how practical duty enriches the
fancy and the heart, and action clears and deep-
ens the affections. Indeed, no one can have a true
idea of right until he does it. No one can have any
genuine reverence for it until he has done it often
and with cost. Also, no one can have any peace inef-
fable in it until he does it always and with alacrity.
Does anyone complain that the best affections are
transient visitors with him, and the heavenly spirit
a stranger to his heart? Oh, let him not go forth, on
any strained wing of thought, in distant quest of
them, but rather stay at home and set his house in
the true order of conscience. Then, of their own accord, the most divine guests will enter.

James Martineau

September 8

Continue in prayer, and watch in the same with thanksgiving. —Colossians 4:2

Watch ye, stand fast in the faith, quit you like men, be strong. —1 Corinthians 16:13

We kneel how weak, we rise how full of power.
Why therefore should we do ourselves this wrong,
Or others—that we are not always strong,
That we are ever overborne with care,
That we should ever weak or heartless be,
Anxious or troubled, when with us is prayer,
And joy and strength and courage are with Thee?
Richard Chenevix Trench

*I*t is impossible for us to make the duties of our situation minister to our sanctification without a habit of devout fellowship with God. This is the spring of all our life, and the strength of it. It is prayer, meditation, and conversation with God that refreshes, restores, and renews the temper of our minds at all times, under all trials, and after all conflicts with the world. By this contact with the world unseen, we receive continual accesses of strength. As our day, so is our strength. Without this healing and refreshing of spirit, duties grow to be burdens, the events of life irritate us, employments lower the tone of our minds, and we become fretful, irritable, and impatient.

Cardinal Henry Edward Manning

*This is a faithful saying, and these things I will that
thou affirm constantly, that they which have believed in
God might be careful to maintain good works.*
—Titus 3:8

Faith's meanest deed more favor bears
Where hearts and wills are weighed,
Than brightest transports, choicest prayers,
Which bloom their hour and fade.
Cardinal John Henry Newman

One secret act of self-denial, one sacrifice of inclination to duty, is worth all the mere good
thoughts, warm feelings, and passionate prayers in
which idle people indulge themselves.
Cardinal John Henry Newman

It is impossible for us to live in fellowship with
God without holiness in all the duties of life. These
things act and react on each other. Without a diligent
and faithful obedience to the calls and claims of others upon us, our religious profession is simply dead.
To disobey conscience when it points to relative duties irritates the whole temper and quenches the first
beginnings of devotion. We cannot go from strife,
breaches, and angry words forward to God. Selfishness, an imperious will, lack of sympathy with the
sufferings and sorrows of other men, neglect of chari-
table offices, suspicions, and hard censures of those
with whom our lot is cast will miserably darken our
own hearts and hide the face of God from us.
Cardinal Henry Edward Manning

Lord, not my feet only, but also my hands and my head.
—John 13:9

Take my hands, and let them move
At the impulse of Thy love.

Take my feet and let them be
Swift and "beautiful" for Thee.

Take my intellect, and use
Every power as Thou shalt choose.

Frances Ridley Havergal

*I*f a man may attain to be unto God as a hand is to a man, let him be content with that and not seek further. That is to say, let him strive and wrestle with all his might to obey God and His commandments so thoroughly at all times and in all things that in him there is nothing, spiritual or natural, that opposes God. Let him strive so, that his whole soul and body, with all their members, may stand ready and willing for that to which God has created them. Let him stand as ready and willing as a hand is to a man, which is so wholly in his power that in the twinkling of an eye, he moves and turns it where he will. And when we find it otherwise with us, we must give our whole diligence to amend our state.

Theologia Germanica

Perfect sanctification is when the mind thinks nothing, when the soul covets nothing, and when the body acts nothing that is contrary to the will of God.

Anonymous, in an old Bible, 1599

September 11

Hallowed be thy name. Thy kingdom come.
—Matthew 6:9–10

The kingdom of established peace,
Which can no more remove;
The perfect powers of godliness,
The omnipotence of love.

Charles Wesley

*M*y child, you may not measure out your offering unto Me by what others have done or left undone. But seek out, even to the last moment of your earthly life, what is the utmost height of pure devotion to which I have called *your own self.* Remember that, if you fall short of this, each time you utter in prayer the words, *"Hallowed be thy name, Thy kingdom come,"* you do most fearfully condemn yourself. For is it not a mockery to ask for what you will not seek to promote even unto the uttermost within the narrow expanse of your own heart and spirit?

The Divine Master

If you do not wish for His kingdom, don't pray for it. But if you do, you must do more than pray for it; you must work for it.

John Ruskin

She obeyed not the voice; she received not correction; she trusted not in the LORD; she drew not near to her God.
—Zephaniah 3:2

Oh! let us not this thought allow;
The heat, the dust upon our brow,
Signs of the contest, we may wear;
Yet thus we shall appear more fair
    In our Almighty Master's eye,
Than if in fear to lose the bloom,
Or ruffle the soul's lightest plume,
    We from the strife should fly.

Richard Chenevix Trench

*I*f God requires anything of us, we have no right to draw back under the pretext that we are liable to commit some fault in obeying. It is better to obey imperfectly than not at all. Perhaps you ought to rebuke someone dependent on you, but you are silent for fear of giving way to vehemence, or you avoid the society of certain persons because they make you cross and impatient. How are you to attain self-control, if you shun all occasions of practicing it? Is not such self-choosing a greater fault than those into which you fear to fall? Aim at a steady mind to do right, go wherever duty calls you, and believe firmly that God will forgive the faults that take your weakness by surprise in spite of your sincere desire to please Him.

Jean Nicolas Grou

It is good that a man should both hope and quietly wait for the salvation of the LORD. —Lamentations 3:26

Truly my soul waiteth upon God: from him cometh my salvation. —Psalm 62:1

> Not so in haste, my heart;
> Have faith in God, and wait;
> Although He linger long,
> He never comes too late.
>
> Anonymous

The true use to be made of all the imperfections of which you are conscious is neither to justify, nor to condemn them, but to present them before God, conforming your will to His and remaining in peace. Peace is the divine order, in whatever state we may be.

Fénelon

You will find it harder to uproot faults than to choke them by gaining virtues. Do not think of your faults; think still less of others' faults. In every person who comes near you, look for what is good and strong. Honor that. Rejoice in it, and, as much as you can, try to imitate it. And then your faults will drop off like dead leaves when their time comes.

John Ruskin

*Call unto me, and I will answer thee, and show thee
great and mighty things, which thou knowest not.*
—Jeremiah 33:3

*And I have also given thee that which thou hast not
asked.* —1 Kings 3:13

No voice of prayer to Thee can rise,
But swift as light Thy Love replies;
Not always what we ask, indeed,
But, O most Kind! what most we need.

Harriet McEwen Kimball

*I*f you have any trial that seems intolerable, pray,
pray that it be relieved or changed. There is no
harm in that. We may pray for anything, not wrong
in itself, with perfect freedom, if we do not pray
selfishly. One disabled from duty by sickness may
pray for health, so that he may do his work. One
hemmed in by internal impediments may pray for
utterance, so that he may serve better the truth and
the right. Or, if we have a troubling sin, we may
pray to be delivered from it, in order to serve God
and man, and not become Satan's to mislead and
destroy. But the answer to the prayer may be, as it
was to Paul, not the removal of the thorn but, instead, a growing insight into its meaning and value.
The voice of God in our souls may show us, as we
look up to Him, that His strength is enough to enable us to bear it.

James Freeman Clarke

September 15

*Can ye drink of the cup that I drink of? and be baptized
with the baptism that I am baptized with?*
—Mark 10:38

> Whate'er my God ordains is right;
> Though I the cup must drink
> That bitter seems to my faint heart,
> I will not fear nor shrink.
>
> Samuel Rodigast

*T*he worst part of martyrdom is not the last agonizing moment. It is the wearing, daily steadfastness. Men who can make up their minds to hold out against the torture of an hour have sunk under the weariness and the annoyance of small, prolonged torments. And there are many Christians who have the weight of some deep, incommunicable grief pressing, cold as ice, upon their hearts. To bear that cheerfully and manfully is to be a martyr. There is many a Christian bereaved and stricken in the best hopes of life. For such a one to say quietly, *"Father...not as I will, but as thou wilt"* (Matt. 26:39), is to be a martyr. There is many a Christian who feels the irksomeness of the duties of life and feels his spirit revolting from them. To get up every morning with the firm resolve to find pleasure in those duties and do them well and finish the work that God has given us to do, that is to drink Christ's cup. The humblest occupation has in it materials of discipline for the highest heaven.

Frederick William Robertson

September 16

Consider the lilies how they grow. —Luke 12:27

> Oh! Source divine, and Life of all,
>> The Fount of Being's fearful sea,
> Thy depth would every heart appall,
>> That saw not love supreme in Thee.
>
> John Sterling

*H*e placed a little thing, the size of a hazelnut, as it seemed to me, in the palm of my hand, and it was as round as a ball. I looked at it with the eye of my understanding and thought, "What may this be?" And I was answered generally thus, "It is all that is made." I marveled how it might last, for I thought it might suddenly have fallen to nothing because it was so small. And I was answered in my understanding, "It lasts, and always will, for God loves it. And so will all things by the love of God." In this little thing I saw three properties. The first is that God made it. The second is that God loves it. The third is that God keeps it. This is why we are not all in ease of heart and soul: because we seek rest here in this thing that is so little, where no rest is. And we do not know our God who is all-mighty, all-wise, and all-good, for He is rest itself. God wills to be known, and it pleases Him that we rest ourselves in Him. For all that is beneath Him, is not enough for us.

Mother Juliana, 1373

Whosoever will be great among you, shall be your minister: and whosoever of you will be the chiefest, shall be servant of all. For even the Son of man came not to be ministered unto, but to minister. —Mark 10:43–45

A child's kiss
Set on thy sighing lips, shall make thee glad;
A poor man served by thee, shall make thee rich;
A sick man helped by thee, shall make thee strong,
Thou shalt be served thyself by every sense
Of service which thou renderest.

Elizabeth Barrett Browning

*L*et every man lovingly cast all his thoughts and cares, and his sins too, as it were, on the will of God. Moreover, if a man, while busy in this lofty inward work, were called by some duty in the providence of God to cease from this work and cook a broth for some sick person, or any other such service, he should do so willingly and with great joy. If I had to forsake such work and go out to preach or anything else, I would go cheerfully. I would not only believe that God would be with me, but that He would grant me that it may be even greater grace and blessing in that external work undertaken out of true love in the service of my neighbor than I should perhaps receive in my season of loftiest contemplation.

John Tauler

All the paths of the LORD are mercy and truth unto such
as keep his covenant and his testimonies.
—Psalm 25:10

Speak Lord, for Thy servant heareth,
Speak peace to my anxious soul,
And help me to feel that all my ways
Are under Thy wise control;

That He who cares for the lily,
And heeds the sparrows' fall,
Shall tenderly lead His loving child:
For He made and loveth all.

Anonymous

*I*t is not by seeking more fertile regions where toil is lighter—happier circumstances free from difficult complications and troublesome people—but by bringing the high courage of a devout soul, clear in principle and aim, to bear upon what is given to us, that we brighten our inward light. Then we can lead something of a true life, and introduce the kingdom of heaven into the midst of our earthly days. If we cannot work out the will of God where God has placed us, then why has He placed us there?

John Hamilton Thom

September 19

Pray for us unto the LORD thy God...that the LORD thy God may show us the way wherein we may walk, and the thing that we may do. —Jeremiah 42:2–3

That which I see not teach thou me. —Job 34:32

> O Father, hear!
> The way is dark, and I would fain discern
> What steps to take, into which path to turn;
> Oh! make it clear.
> *Christian Intelligencer*

*W*e can't choose happiness either for ourselves or for another. We can't tell where that will lie. We can only choose whether we will indulge ourselves in the present moment or whether we will renounce that, for the sake of obeying the divine voice within us, for the sake of being true to all the motives that sanctify our lives. I know this belief is hard. It has slipped away from me again and again, but I have felt that if I let it go forever, I would have no light through the darkness of this life.

George Eliot

There was a concern on my mind to pass my time in such a way that nothing might hinder me from the steadiest attention to the voice of the true Shepherd.

John Woolman

Thou shalt hide them in the secret of thy presence from the pride of man: thou shalt keep them secretly in a pavilion from the strife of tongues. —Psalm 31:20

> The praying spirit breathe,
>   The watching power impart,
> From all entanglements beneath
>   Call off my anxious heart.
> My feeble mind sustain,
>   By worldly thoughts oppressed;
> Appear, and bid me turn again
>   To my eternal rest.

Charles Wesley

If you could once make up your mind in the fear of God never to undertake more work of any sort than you can carry on calmly, quietly, and without hurry or flurry, you would find this simple commonsense rule doing for you what no prayers or tears could ever accomplish. The instant you feel yourself growing nervous and like one out of breath, you should stop and take a breath.

Elizabeth Prentiss

As soon as we are with God in faith and in love, we are in prayer.

Fénelon

How excellent is thy lovingkindness, O God! therefore the children of men put their trust under the shadow of thy wings. —Psalm 36:7

The eternal God is thy refuge, and underneath are the everlasting arms. —Deuteronomy 33:27

> Within Thy circling arms we lie,
> O God! in Thy infinity:
> Our souls in quiet shall abide,
> Beset with love on every side.
>
> Anonymous

*T*he everlasting arms." I think of that whenever rest is sweet. How the whole earth and the almighty strength of it are beneath every tired creature to give it rest, holding us, always! No thought of God is closer than that. No human tenderness of patience is greater than that which gathers in its arms a little child and holds it, heedless of weariness. And He fills the great earth, and all upon it, with this unseen force of His love, that never forgets or exhausts itself, so that everywhere we may lie down in His bosom and be comforted.

Adeline D. T. Whitney

The word is very nigh unto thee, in thy mouth, and in thy heart, that thou mayest do it. —Deuteronomy 30:14

> But, above all, the victory is most sure
> For him, who, seeking faith by virtue, strives
> To yield entire obedience to the Law
> Of Conscience; Conscience reverenced and obeyed,
> As God's most intimate presence in the soul,
> And His most perfect image in the world.
>
> William Wordsworth

*W*hat we call conscience is the voice of divine love in the deep of our beings. It desires union with our wills. And by attracting the affections inward, conscience invites them to enter into the harmonious contentment and *"fulness of joy"* (Ps. 16:11), which attends the being joined by one spirit to the Lord (1 Cor. 6:17).

James Pierrepoint Greaves

I rejoice that God has bestowed upon you a relish and inclination for the inner life. To be called to this precious and lofty life is a great and undeserved grace of God, to which we ought to respond with great faithfulness. God invites us to His fellowship of love and wishes to prepare our spirit to be His own abode and temple.

Gerhard Tersteegen

Show me thy ways, O LORD; teach me thy paths.
—Psalm 25:4

> When we cannot see our way,
> Let us trust and still obey;
> He who bids us forward go,
> Cannot fail the way to show.
> Though the sea be deep and wide,
> Though a passage seem denied;
> Fearless let us still proceed,
> Since the Lord vouchsafes to lead.
>
> Anonymous

*T*here is nothing like the first glance we get at duty before there has been any special pleading of our affections or inclinations. Duty is never uncertain at first. It is only after we have gotten involved in the mazes and fallacies of wishing that things were otherwise than they are, that it seems indistinct. Considering a duty is often only explaining it away. Deliberation is often only dishonesty. God's guidance is plain, when we are true.

Frederick William Robertson

That which is often asked of God is not so much His will and way, as His approval of our way.

Sarah F. Smiley

When I awake, I am still with thee. —Psalm 139:18

> Let the glow of love destroy
> Cold obedience faintly given;
> Wake our hearts to strength and joy
> With the flushing eastern heaven.
> Let us truly rise, ere yet
> > Life be set.

Christian Knorr von Rosenroth

*W*ith his first waking consciousness he can set himself to take a serious, manly view of the day before him. He ought to know pretty well in what areas his difficulty is likely to come, whether in being irritable or domineering or sharp in his bargains or self-absorbed or whatever it may be. Now, in this quiet hour, he can take a good, full look at his enemy and make up his mind to beat him. It is a good time, too, for giving his thoughts a range quite beyond himself, beyond even his own moral struggles. It is a good time, there in the stillness, for going into the realm of other lives. His wife—what needs does she have for help, for sympathy, that he can meet? His children—how can he make the day sweeter to them? This acquaintance who is having a hard time; this friend, who dropped a word to you yesterday that you hardly noticed in your hurry, but that comes up to you now, revealing in him some finer trait, some deeper hunger, than you had guessed before—now you can think these things over. So, you get your day somewhat into right perspective and proportion before you begin it.

George Spring Merriam

Ye shall rejoice in all that ye put your hand unto, ye and your households, wherein the LORD thy God hath blessed thee. —Deuteronomy 12:7

Sweet is the smile of home; the mutual look
When hearts are of each other sure;
Sweet all the joys that crowd the household nook,
The haunts of all affections pure.

John Keble

*I*s there any tie that absence has loosened, or that the wear and tear of everyday dealings, little uncongenialities, unconfessed misunderstandings, have fretted into the heart, until it bears something of the nature of a fetter? Is there any cup at our home table whose sweetness we have not fully tasted, although it might yet make a continual feast of our daily bread? Let us evaluate these treasures while they are still ours, in thankfulness to God.

Elizabeth Charles

We ought daily or weekly to dedicate a little time to the evaluation of the virtues of our belongings—wife, children, friends—and to the contemplation of them then in a beautiful group. And we should do so now, so that we may not pardon and love in vain and too late, after the beloved one has been taken away from us to a better world.

Jean Paul Richter

Yea, though I walk through the valley of the shadow of death, I will fear no evil: for thou art with me; thy rod and thy staff they comfort me. —Psalm 23:4

O Will, that willest good alone,
  Lead Thou the way, Thou guidest best;
A silent child, I follow on,
  And trusting lean upon Thy breast.
And if in gloom I see Thee not,
  I lean upon Thy love unknown;
In me Thy blessed will is wrought,
  If I will nothing of my own.

Gerhard Tersteegen

*T*he devout soul is always safe in every state, if it makes everything an occasion either of rising up or falling down into the hands of God. And it is safe if it is exercising faith and trust and resignation to Him. The pious soul that eyes only God, that means to be nothing but His alone, can have no stop put to its progress. Light and darkness equally assist him. In the light he looks up to God. In the darkness he lays hold of God. And so they both do him the same good.

William Law

September 27

When I sit in darkness, the LORD shall be a light unto me. —Micah 7:8

There be many that say, Who will show us any good? LORD, lift thou up the light of thy countenance upon us.
—Psalm 4:6

How oft a gleam of glory sent
    Straight through the deepest, darkest night,
    Has filled the soul with heavenly light,
With holy peace and sweet content.

Anonymous

Suppose you are bewildered and do not know what is right or what is true. Can you not cease to regard whether you do or not, whether you are bewildered, whether you are happy? Can you not love utterly and perfectly, and rejoice to be in the dark and beset by gloom, because that very thing is the fact of God's infinite being? Can you not take this trial also into your own heart and be ignorant, not because you are obliged, but because it is God's will, it is yours also? Do you not see that a person who truly loves is united with the Infinite Being and cannot be uncomfortable or unhappy? It is that which *is* that he wills and desires and holds best of all to be. To know God is utterly to sacrifice self.

James Hinton

My little children, let us not love in word, neither in tongue; but in deed and in truth. —1 John 3:18

But be ye doers of the word, and not hearers only, deceiving your own selves. —James 1:22

Thrice blest whose lives are faithful prayers,
    Whose loves in higher love endure;
    What souls possess themselves so pure,
Or is there blessedness like theirs?

Alfred Tennyson

Let every creature have your love. Love, with its fruits of meekness, patience, and humility, is all that we can wish for ourselves and our fellow creatures. For this is to live in God, united with Him, both for time and eternity. To desire to communicate good to everyone, in the degree that we can and to which each person is capable of receiving from us, is a divine temper, for thus God stands unchangeably disposed towards the whole creation.

William Law

What will be our reward for loving our neighbor as ourselves in this life? That when we become angels, we will be enabled lo love him better than ourselves.

Emanuel Swedenborg

Blessed are the pure in heart: for they shall see God.
—Matthew 5:8

Follow peace with all men, and holiness, without which no man shall see the Lord. —Hebrews 12:14

Since Thou Thyself dost still display
Unto the pure in heart,
Oh, make us children of the day
To know Thee as Thou art.
For Thou art light and life and love;
And Thy redeemed below
May see Thee as Thy saints above,
And know Thee as they know.

James Montgomery

Doubt, gloom, and impatience have been expelled. Joy has taken their place: the hope of heaven and the harmony of a pure heart, the triumph of self-mastery, sober thoughts, and a contented mind. How can charity towards all men fail to follow, being the mere inclination of innocence and peace? Thus the Spirit of God creates in us the simplicity and warmth of heart that children have. Not only this, but He also creates in us the perfections of His heavenly hosts, high and low being joined together in His mysterious work. For, what are implicit trust, ardent love, abiding purity, except the mind both of little children and of the adoring seraphim!

Cardinal John Henry Newman

LORD, who shall abide in thy tabernacle? who shall dwell in thy holy hill? He that walketh uprightly, and worketh righteousness, and speaketh the truth in his heart. —Psalm 15:1–2

How happy is he born or taught,
That serveth not another's will,
Whose armor is his honest thought,
And simple truth his utmost skill.

Sir Henry Wotton

*I*f you work at that which is before you, you will live happily. You need to be following what is right and reasonable, seriously, vigorously, calmly, without allowing anything else to distract you. And you should be keeping your divine part pure as if you are bound to give it back immediately. If you hold to this, expecting nothing, fearing nothing, but being satisfied with your present activity according to nature, and with heroic truth in every word and sound that you utter, a happy life is possible. And there is no man who is able to prevent this.

Marcus Aurelius Antoninus

*Be strong, all ye people of the land, saith the LORD, and
work: for I am with you, saith the LORD of hosts.*
                    —Haggai 2:4

> Yet the world is Thy field, Thy garden;
>   On earth art Thou still at home.
> When Thou bendest hither Thy hallowing eye,
> My narrow workroom seems vast and high,
> Its dingy ceiling a rainbow dome—
> Stand ever thus at my wide-swung door,
>   And toil will be toil no more.
>
> Lucy Larcom

*T*he situation that does not have its duty, its
ideal, was never yet occupied by man. Yes,
here, in this poor, miserable, hampered, despicable
place, in which you even now stand, here or nowhere is your ideal. Work it out from this. And
working, believe, live, and be free. Fool! The ideal is
in yourself. The impediment, too, is in yourself.
Your condition is simply the stuff you are to shape
that same ideal out of. What does it matter whether
such stuff is of this sort or that, or the form you give
it is heroic or poetic. Oh, you who pine in the im-
prisonment of the actual and cry bitterly to the gods
for a kingdom in which to rule and create, know this
to be a truth: the thing you seek is already with you,
here or nowhere, if you could only see!

Thomas Carlyle

October 2

I am purposed that my mouth shall not transgress.
—Psalm 17:3

In the multitude of words there wanteth not sin: but he that refraineth his lips is wise. —Proverbs 10:19

> Prune thou thy words; the thoughts control
> That o'er thee swell and throng;
> They will condense within thy soul,
> And change to purpose strong.
> Cardinal John Henry Newman

*F*ew men suspect how much mere talk fritters away spiritual energy. That which should be spent in action, spends itself in words. Hence he who restrains that love of talk lays up a fund of spiritual strength.

Frederick William Robertson

Do not flatter yourself that your thoughts are under due control, your desires properly regulated, or your dispositions subject as they should be to Christian principle, if your discourse with others consists mainly of frivolous gossip, impertinent anecdotes, speculations on the character and affairs of your neighbors, the repetition of former conversations, or a discussion of the current petty scandal of society. Much less are your thoughts under control if you allow yourself careless exaggeration on all these points and that grievous inattention to exact truth, which is apt to accompany the statements of those whose conversation is made up of these materials.

Henry Ware, Jr.

Judge not, that ye be not judged. —Matthew 7:1

Why beholdest thou the mote that is in thy brother's eye, but perceivest not the beam that is in thine own eye?
—Luke 6:41

Judge not; the workings of his brain
    And of his heart thou canst not see;
What looks to thy dim eyes a stain,
    In God's pure light may only be
A scar, brought from some well-won field,
Where thou wouldst only faint and yield.

                       Adelaide Anne Procter

When you behold an aspect for whose constant gloom and frown you cannot account, whose unvarying cloud exasperates you by its apparent causelessness, be sure that there is a canker somewhere. It is a canker not the less deeply corroding because it is concealed.

                       Charlotte Brontë

While we are coldly discussing a man's career, sneering at his mistakes, blaming his rashness, and labeling his opinions—"evangelical and narrow," or "liberal and pantheistic," or "Anglican and egotistic"—that man, in his solitude, is perhaps shedding hot tears because his sacrifice is a hard one. His strength and patience may be failing him to speak the difficult word and do the difficult deed.

                       George Eliot

*Be strong and of a good courage; be not afraid, neither
be thou dismayed: for the LORD thy God is with thee
whithersoever thou goest.* —Joshua 1:9

By Thine unerring Spirit led,
    We shall not in the desert stray;
We shall not full direction need,
    Nor miss our providential way;
As far from danger as from fear,
While love, almighty love, is near.

Charles Wesley

*W*atch your way then, as a cautious traveler.
Don't be gazing at that mountain and river
in the distance and saying, "How will I ever get over
them?" But, keep to the present little inch that is
before you, and accomplish in the little moment
what belongs to it. The mountain and the river can
only be passed in the same way, and when you come
to them, you will come to the light and strength that
belong to them.

Mary Anne Kelty

Do not let future things disturb you, for you
will come to them, if it will be necessary, having
with you the same reason that you now use for present
things.

Marcus Aurelius Antoninus

October 5

Say to them that are of a fearful heart, Be strong, fear not. —Isaiah 35:4

> Why shouldst thou fill today with sorrow
> About tomorrow,
> My heart?
> One watches all with care most true,
> Doubt not that He will give thee too
> Thy part.
>
> Paul Flemming

The crosses that we make for ourselves by a restless anxiety as to the future, are not crosses that come from God. We show lack of faith in Him by our false wisdom, wishing to forestall His arrangements, and struggling to supplement His providence by our own providence. The future is not yet ours. Perhaps it never will be. If it comes, it may come wholly different from what we have foreseen. Let us shut our eyes, then, to that which God hides from us and keeps in reserve in the treasures of His deep counsels. Let us worship without seeing. Let us be silent and abide in peace.

Fénelon

I had fainted, unless I had believed to see the goodness of the LORD in the land of the living. —Psalm 27:13

I will surely do thee good. —Genesis 32:12

Thou know'st not what is good for thee,
But God doth know,—
Let Him thy strong reliance be,
And rest thee so.
Christian Fürchtegott Gellert

Let us be very careful of thinking, on the one hand, that we have no work assigned us to do or, on the other hand, that what we have assigned to us is not the right thing for us. If ever we can say in our hearts to God, in reference to any daily duty, "This is not my place. I would choose something dearer. I am capable of something higher," we are guilty not only of rebellion, but also of blasphemy. It is equivalent to saying not only, "My heart revolts against Your commands," but also, "Your commands are unwise. Your almighty guidance is unskillful. Your omniscient eye has mistaken the capacities of Your creature. Your infinite love is indifferent to the welfare of Your child."
Elizabeth Charles

October 7

And because ye are sons, God hath sent forth the Spirit of his Son into your hearts, crying, Abba, Father.
—Galatians 4:6

O Lord, forgive my sin,
And deign to put within
A calm, obedient heart, a patient mind;
That I may murmur not,
Though bitter seem my lot;
For hearts unthankful can no blessing find.

Rutilius

Resignation to the divine will signifies a cheerful admiration and thankful acceptance of everything that comes from God. It is not enough patiently to submit, but we must thankfully receive and fully approve of everything that, by the order of God's providence, happens to us. For there is no reason why we should be patient, except what is as good and as strong a reason why we should be thankful. Therefore, whenever you find yourself disposed to uneasiness or murmuring at anything that is the effect of God's providence over you, you must look upon yourself as denying either the wisdom or the goodness of God.

William Law

Ye shall not go out with haste, nor go by flight: for the LORD will go before you; and the God of Israel will be your rereward. —Isaiah 52:12

He that believeth shall not make haste. —Isaiah 28:16

> Holy Spirit, Peace divine!
> Still this restless heart of mine;
> Speak to calm this tossing sea,
> Stayed in Thy tranquillity.
>
> Samuel Longfellow

*I*n whatever you are called upon to do, endeavor to maintain a calm, collected, and prayerful state of mind. Self-recollection is of great importance. *"It is good that a man should...quietly wait for the salvation of the LORD"* (Lam. 3:26). He who is in what may be called a spiritual hurry, or rather who runs without having evidence of being spiritually sent, makes haste to no purpose.

Thomas Cogswell Upham

There is great fret and worry in always searching for more work. It is not good intellectually or spiritually.

Annie Keary

Whenever we are outwardly excited we should cease to act, but whenever we have a message from the spirit within, we should execute it with calmness. A fine day may excite one to act, but it is much better that we act from the calm spirit in any day, be the outward what it may.

James Pierrepoint Greaves

As for me and my house, we will serve the LORD.
—Joshua 24:15

O happy house! and happy servitude!
    Where all alike one Master own;
Where daily duty, in thy strength pursued,
    Is never hard or toilsome known;
Where each one serves Thee, meek and lowly,
    Whatever Thine appointment be,
Till common tasks seem great and holy,
    When they are done as unto Thee.

                  Carl Johann Philipp Spitta

*A*t Dudson there was no rushing after anything, either worldly or intellectual. It was a home of constant activity, issuing from, and retiring to, a center of deep repose. There was an earnest application of excellent sense to the daily duties of life, to the minutest courtesy and kindness, as well as to the real interests of others. Everything great and everything little seemed done in the same spirit, and with the same degree of fidelity, because it was the will of God, and that which could not be traced to His will was not undertaken at all. Nothing at Dudson was esteemed too little to be cared for, and nothing too great to be undertaken at the command of God. For this they daily exercised their mental and bodily powers on the things around them, knowing that our Lord thoroughly furnishes each of His soldiers for his work and places before each the task he has to do.

                  Mary Anne Schimmelpenninck

Now the Lord of peace himself give you peace always by all means. —2 Thessalonians 3:16

The LORD will give strength unto his people; the LORD will bless his people with peace. —Psalm 29:11

In the heart's depths a peace serene and holy
    Abides, and when pain seems to have its will,
Or we despair,—oh, may that peace rise slowly,
    Stronger than agony, and we be still.

Samuel Johnson

*B*ut if a man ought and is willing to lie still under God's hand, he must and ought also to lie still under all things, whether they come from God, himself, or any creature, nothing excepted. And he who would be obedient, resigned, and submissive to God must and ought to be also resigned, obedient, and submissive to all things, in a spirit of yielding and not of resistance. He should take them in silence, resting on the hidden foundations of his soul. He should have a secret inward patience that enables him to take all chances or crosses willingly. Whatever befalls him, he is neither to call for nor desire any redress or deliverance or resistance or revenge, but he is always to cry in a loving, sincere humility, *"Father, forgive them; for they know not what they do"* (Luke 23:34).

Theologia Germanica

And when the people complained, it displeased the LORD. —Numbers 11:1

> When thou hast thanked thy God
> For every blessing sent,
> What time will then remain
> For murmurs or lament?
>
> Richard Chenevix Trench

Let him, with a cheerful and thankful spirit, yield himself up to suffer whatever God will appoint to him. And let him fulfill, according to his power, by the grace of God, all His holy will to the utmost that he can discern it. Never let him complain of his distresses except to God alone with entire and humble resignation, praying that he may be strong to endure all his sufferings according to the will of God.

John Tauler

He who complains, or thinks he has a right to complain, because he is called in God's providence to suffer, has something within him that needs to be taken away. A soul whose will is lost in God's will can never do this. Sorrow may exist, but complaint never.

Catherine Adorna

October 12

Singing and making melody in your heart to the Lord.
—Ephesians 5:19

Sanctify the Lord God in your hearts. —1 Peter 3:15

There are in this loud stunning tide
    Of human care and crime,
With whom the melodies abide
    Of th' everlasting chime;
Who carry music in their heart
Through dusky lane and wrangling mart,
Plying their daily task with busier feet,
Because their secret souls a holy strain repeat.

John Keble

Strive to carry yourself with a total resignation to the divine will, so that God may do with you and all yours according to His heavenly pleasure, relying on Him as on a kind and loving Father. Never revoke that intention, and though you are concerned with the affairs of the condition in which God has placed you, you will still be in prayer, in the presence of God, and in perpetual acts of resignation. "A just man leaves not off to pray unless he leaves off to be just." He who always does well always prays. The good desire is prayer, and if the desire is continued, so also is the prayer.

Miguel Molinos

We desire that every one of you do show the same diligence to the full assurance of hope unto the end.
—Hebrews 6:11

The Lord is faithful, who shall stablish you, and keep you from evil. —2 Thessalonians 3:3

> Long though my task may be,
>   Cometh the end.
> God 't is that helpeth me,
> His is the work, and He
>   New strength will lend.

Anonymous.

*S*et yourself steadfastly to those duties which have the least attractive exterior. It does not matter whether God's holy will is fulfilled in great or small matters. Be patient with yourself and your own failings. Never be in a hurry, and do not yield to longings for that which is impossible to you. My dear sister, go on steadily and quietly. If our dear Lord means you to run, He will *"strengthen your heart"* (Ps. 31:24).

Francis de Sales

Always begin by doing that which costs you most, unless the easier duty is a pressing one. Examine, classify, and determine at night the work of tomorrow. Arrange things in the order of their importance, and act accordingly. Dread, above all things, bitterness and irritation. Never say, or indirectly recall, anything to your advantage.

Madame Anne Sophie Swetchine

He that sinneth against me wrongeth his own soul: all they that hate me love death. —Proverbs 8:36

But now being made free from sin, and become servants to God, ye have your fruit unto holiness, and the end everlasting life. For the wages of sin is death; but the gift of God is eternal life through Jesus Christ our Lord. —Romans 6:22–23

O Sovereign Love, to Thee I cry!
Give me Thyself, or else I die!
Save me from death; from hell set free!
Death, hell, are but the want of Thee.
Quickened by Thy imparted flame,
Saved when possessed of Thee, I am:
My life, my only heaven Thou art;
O might I feel Thee in my heart!

Charles Wesley

Sin itself is hell and death and misery to the soul, as being a departure from goodness and holiness itself, I mean from God, in conjunction with whom the happiness and blessedness and heaven of a soul consist. Avoid it, therefore, as you would avoid being miserable.

Samuel Shaw

I couldn't live in peace if I put the shadow of a willful sin between myself and God.

George Eliot

Unholy tempers are always unhappy tempers.
John Wesley

Mine iniquities have taken hold upon me, so that I am not able to look up;...therefore my heart faileth me. Be pleased, O LORD, to deliver me: O LORD, make haste to help me. —Psalm 40:12–13

Sin shall not have dominion over you. —Romans 6:14

O Thou, to whose all-searching sight
The darkness shineth as the light!
Search, prove my heart; it pants for Thee:
Oh, burst these bonds, and set it free!

Gerhard Tersteegen

Yes, this sin that has sent me weary-hearted to bed and desperate in heart to morning work, can be conquered. It may have made my plans miscarry until I am a coward, cut me off from prayer, robbed the sky of blueness and the earth of springtime and the air of freshness and human faces of friendliness. This blasting sin that perhaps has made my bed in hell for me so long—this can be conquered. I do not say annihilated, but, better than that, conquered, captured, and transfigured into a friend. So, I at last shall say, "My temptation has become my strength! For to the very fight with it I owe my force."

William Channing Gannett

*I am not worthy of the least of all the mercies, and of all
the truth, which thou hast showed unto thy servant.*
—Genesis 32:10

Some murmur if their sky is clear,
    And wholly bright to view,
If one small speck of dark appear
    In their great heaven of blue:
And some with thankful love are filled,
    If but one streak of light,
One ray of God's good mercy, gild
    The darkness of their night.
Richard Chenevix Trench

*H*abitual sufferers are precisely those who least frequently doubt the divine benevolence and whose faith and love rise to the serenest cheerfulness. Possessed by no idea of a prescriptive right to be happy, their blessings are not befuddled by anticipation, but come to them fresh and brilliant as the first day's morning and evening light came to the dwellers in Paradise. With the happy, it is their constant peace that seems to come by nature, and to be blunted by its commonness. Then their griefs seem to come from God, sharpened by their sacred origin. With the sufferer, it is his pain that appears to be a thing of course, and to require no explanation. His relief, then, is reverently welcomed as a divine interposition and, as a breath of heaven, caresses the heart into melodies of praise.
James Martineau

Hath the LORD as great delight in burnt offerings and sacrifices, as in obeying the voice of the LORD? Behold, to obey is better than sacrifice. —1 Samuel 15:22

Fear ye not, stand still, and see the salvation of the LORD, which he will show to you to day.
—Exodus 14:13

The folded hands seem idle:
If folded at His word,
'T is a holy service, trust me,
In obedience to the Lord.

Anna Shipton

*I*t is not the multitude of hard duties, it is not constraint and contention that advance us in our Christian course. On the contrary, it is the yielding of our wills without restriction and without choice to tread cheerfully every day in the path in which Providence leads us. It is to seek nothing, to be discouraged by nothing, to see our duty in the present moment, and to trust all else without reserve to the will and power of God.

Fénelon

Godliness is the devotion of the soul to God, as to a living person whose will is to be its law, whose love is to be its life. It is the habit of living before the face of God, and not simply doing certain things.

James Baldwin Brown

October 18

Except your righteousness shall exceed the righteous-ness of the scribes and Pharisees, ye shall in no case enter into the kingdom of heaven. —Matthew 5:20

> The freedom from all willful sin,
>   The Christian's daily task,
> Oh these are graces far below
>   What longing love would ask!
> Dole not thy duties out to God.
>
>   Frederick William Faber

*Y*ou perhaps will say that all people fall short of the perfection of the Gospel, and therefore you are content with your failings. But this is saying nothing to the purpose, for the question is not whether gospel perfection can be fully attained, but whether you come as near it as a sincere intention and careful diligence can carry you. It is whether you are not in a much lower state than you might be if you sincerely intended, and carefully labored, to advance yourself in all Christian virtues.

                                          William Law

We do not know exactly how low the least degree of obedience is, which will bring a man to heaven, but this we are quite sure of, that he who aims no higher will be sure to fall short even of that, and that he who goes farthest beyond it will be most blessed.

                                          John Keble

Thus saith the LORD, thy Redeemer, the Holy One of Israel; I am the LORD thy God which teacheth thee to profit, which leadeth thee by the way that thou shouldest go. —Isaiah 48:17

> I seek Thy aid, I ask direction,
>   Teach me to do what pleaseth Thee;
> I can bear toil, endure affliction,
>   Only thy leadings let me see.

Anonymous

Of all paths a man could strike into, there is, at any given moment, a best path for every man. There is a thing that, here and now, would of all things be wisest for him to do; and if he could be led or driven to do it, he would then be "like a man," as we phrase it. His success, in such a case, would be complete, his felicity a maximum. This path, to find this path and walk in it, is the one thing necessary for him.

Thomas Carlyle

Every man has his own vocation. There is one direction in which all space is open to him. He has faculties silently inviting him there to endless exertion. He is like a ship in a river. He runs against obstructions on every side but one. On that side all obstruction is taken away, and he sweeps serenely over a deepening channel into an infinite sea.

Ralph Waldo Emerson

Be not overcome of evil, but overcome evil with good.
—Romans 12:21

> Come, in this accepted hour;
> Bring Thy heavenly kingdom in;
> Fill us with Thy glorious power,
> Rooting out the seeds of sin.
> Charles Wesley

*I*f we wish to overcome evil, we must overcome it with good. There are doubtless many ways of overcoming the evil in our own hearts, but the simplest, easiest, and most universal way is to overcome it by active occupation in some good word or work. The best antidote against evil of all kinds, against the evil thoughts that haunt the soul, against the needless perplexities that distract the conscience, is to keep hold of the good we have. Impure thoughts will not stand against pure words and prayers and deeds. Little doubts will not avail against great certainties. Fix your affections on things above, and then you will be less and less troubled by the cares, the temptations, and the troubles of things on earth.

Arthur Penrhyn Stanley

October 21

I am the Almighty God; walk before me, and be thou perfect. —Genesis 17:1

Consecrate yourselves to day to the LORD. —Exodus 32:29

Take my life, and let it be
Consecrated, Lord, to Thee.

Take my moments and my days;
Let them flow in ceaseless praise.

Frances Ridley Havergal

I have noticed that wherever there has been a faithful following of the Lord in a consecrated soul, several things have inevitably followed, sooner or later. Meekness and quietness of spirit become in time the characteristics of the daily life. Many graces are invariably found to be the natural outward development of that inward life which is hid with Christ in God. These graces include the following: a submissive acceptance of the will of God as it comes in the hourly events of each day; pliability in the hands of God to do or to allow all the good pleasure of His will; sweetness under provocation; calmness in the midst of turmoil and bustle; yieldingness to the wishes of others, and an insensibility to slights and affronts; absence of worry or anxiety; deliverance from care and fear.

Hannah Whitall Smith

October 22

Just as Thou wilt is just what I would will;
Give me but this, the heart to be content,
And, if my wish is thwarted, to lie still,
Waiting till puzzle and till pain are spent,
And the sweet thing made plain which the Lord meant.
Susan Coolidge

Let your will be one with His will, and be glad to be disposed of by Him. He will order all things for you. What can cross your will when it is one with His will, on which all creation hangs, around which all things revolve? Keep your hearts clear of evil thoughts, for as evil choices estrange the will from His will, so evil thoughts cloud the soul and hide Him from us. Whatever sets us in opposition to Him makes our will an intolerable torment. So long as we will one thing and He another, we go on piercing ourselves through and through with a perpetual wound, and His will advances, moving on in sanctity and majesty, crushing ours into the dust.
Cardinal Henry Edward Manning

October 23

Teach me to do thy will; for thou art my God: thy spirit is good; lead me into the land of uprightness.
—Psalm 143:10

The battle of our life is won,
And heaven begun,
When we can say, "Thy will be done!"
But, Lord, until
These restless hearts in Thy deep love are still,
We pray Thee, "Teach us how to do Thy will!"

Lucy Larcom

*Y*ou are seeking your own will. You are seeking some other good than the law you are bound to obey. But how will you find good? It is not a thing of choice. It is a river that flows from the foot of the invisible throne and flows by the path of obedience. I say again, man cannot choose his duties. You may choose to forsake your duties and choose not to have the sorrow they bring. But you will go forth, and what will you find? Sorrow without duty—bitter herbs, and no bread with them.

George Eliot

However dark and profitless, however painful and weary, existence may have become, life is not done when we still have duties to do. However any man, like Elijah, may be tempted to cast himself down beneath the juniper tree and say, *"It is enough; now, O LORD"* (1 Kings 19:4), our Christian character is not won, so long as God has anything left for us to suffer or anything left for us to do.

Frederick William Robertson

The LORD is my strength and my shield; my heart
trusted in him, and I am helped: therefore my heart
greatly rejoiceth; and with my song will I praise him.
—Psalm 28:7

Well may Thy happy children cease
    From restless wishes, prone to sin,
And, in Thy own exceeding peace,
    Yield to Thy daily discipline.

Anna Laetitia Waring

*T*alk of haircloth shirts and scourgings and sleeping on ashes, as means of saintship! There is no need of them in our country. Let a woman once look at her domestic trials as her haircloth, her ashes, her scourges. Let her accept them, rejoice in them, smile and be quiet, silent, patient, and loving under them, and the convent can teach her no more. She is a victorious saint.

Harriet Beecher Stowe

Perhaps it is a greater energy of Divine Providence that keeps the Christian from day to day, from year to year, that maintains him as a living martyr, than that which bears him up for an hour in sacrificing himself at the stake. It keeps him praying, hoping, running, and believing against all hindrances.

Richard Cecil

For I am persuaded, that neither death, nor life, nor angels, nor principalities, nor powers, nor things present, nor things to come, nor height, nor depth, nor any other creature, shall be able to separate us from the love of God, which is in Christ Jesus our Lord.
—Romans 8:38–39

I know not what the future hath
Of marvel or surprise,
Assured alone that life and death
His mercy underlies.
John Greenleaf Whittier

*B*e of good faith, my dear friends. Do not look out at anything. Fear none of those things you may be exposed to suffer, either outwardly or inwardly. But trust the Lord over all, and your life will spring and grow and refresh you. And, you will learn obedience and faithfulness daily more and more, even by your exercises and sufferings. Yes, the Lord will teach you the very mystery of faith and obedience, the wisdom, power, love, and goodness of the Lord ordering everything for you, and ordering your hearts in everything.

Isaac Penington

Turn you to the strong hold, ye prisoners of hope.
        —Zechariah 9:12

Their strength is to sit still. —Isaiah 30:7

O power to do; O baffled will!
        O prayer and action! ye are one.
Who may not strive, may yet fulfill
The harder task of standing still,
        And good but wished with God is done.
                                John Greenleaf Whittier

That God has limited our lives may add a peculiar element of trial. Often, though, it defines our way and cuts off many tempting possibilities that perplex the free and the strong, while it leaves intact the whole body of spiritual reality related to the beatitude: if we know these things, happy are we if we do them (John 13:17). We know that God orders the lot. To meet it with the energies it requires and permits, neither more nor less, is what we have to do. We have to fill it at every available point with the light and action of an earnest and spiritually inventive mind, though its scene is no wider than a sick chamber and its action narrowed to patient suffering. We have to meet it with gentle and cheerful words, and all the light it can emit with the thankful quiet of a trustful eye. We must do this without chafing as though God had misjudged our sphere and placed us wrongly and did not know where we could best serve Him.

                                John Hamilton Thom

*Therefore I take pleasure in infirmities, in reproaches,
in necessities, in persecutions, in distresses for Christ's
sake: for when I am weak, then am I strong.*
—2 Corinthians 12:10

Whate'er God does is well!
In patience let us wait;
He doth Himself our burdens bear,
    He doth for us take care,
And He, our God, knows all our weary days.
    Come, give Him praise.

Benjamin Schmolcke

*N*othing else but seeing God in everything will
make us loving and patient with those who
annoy and trouble us. They will then be to us only
the instruments for accomplishing His tender and
wise purposes towards us, and we will even find
ourselves at last inwardly thanking them for the
blessings they bring us. Nothing else will completely
put an end to all murmuring or rebelling thoughts.

Hannah Whitall Smith

The subjection of the will is accomplished by
calmly resigning yourself in everything that inter-
nally or externally disturbs you, for it is thus only
that the soul is prepared for the reception of divine
influences. Prepare the heart like clean paper, and
the Divine Wisdom will imprint on it characters to
His own liking.

Miguel Molinos

I know the thoughts that I think toward you, saith the LORD, thoughts of peace, and not of evil, to give you an expected end. —Jeremiah 29:11

Thy thoughts are good, and Thou art kind,
    E'en when we think it not;
How many an anxious, faithless mind
    Sits grieving o'er its lot,
And frets, and pines by day and night,
As God had lost it out of sight,
    And all its wants forgot.

Paul Gerhardt

You are never to complain of your birth, your training, your employments, your hardships. You are never to fancy that you could be something if only you had a different lot and sphere assigned to you. God understands His own plan, and He knows what you need a great deal better than you do. The very things that you most seek to avert, as fatal limitations or obstructions, are probably what you most need. What you call hindrances, obstacles, or discouragements, are probably God's opportunities. Bring down your soul, or, rather, bring it up to receive God's will and do His work, in your lot, in your sphere, under your cloud of obscurity, and against your temptations. Then you will find that your condition is never opposed to your good, but is really consistent with it.

Horace Bushnell

Behold, I have refined thee, but not with silver; I have chosen thee in the furnace of affliction. —Isaiah 48:10

Be patient, suffering soul! I hear thy cry.
The trial fires may glow, but I am nigh.
    I see the silver, and I will refine
    Until My image shall upon it shine.
Fear not, for I am near, thy help to be;
Greater than all thy pain, My love for thee.

H. W. C.

God takes a thousand times more pains with us than the artist with his picture. By many touches of sorrow and by many colors of circumstances He would bring man into the form that is the highest and noblest in His sight, if only we would receive His gifts and myrrh in the right spirit. But when the cup is put away, and these feelings are stifled or unheeded, a greater injury is done to the soul than can ever be amended. For no heart can conceive in what surpassing love God gives us this myrrh. Yet this, which we ought to receive to our soul's good, we allow to pass by us in our sleepy indifference, and nothing comes of it. Then we come and complain, "Alas, Lord! I am so dry, and it is so dark within me!" I tell you, dear child, open your heart to the pain, and it will do you more good than if you were full of feeling and devoutness.

John Tauler

That good thing which was committed unto thee keep by the Holy Ghost which dwelleth in us.
—2 Timothy 1:14

Oh that the Comforter would come!
Nor visit as a transient guest,
But fix in me His constant home,
And keep possession of my breast:
And make my soul His loved abode,
The temple of indwelling God!

Charles Wesley

Your spirit should become, while yet on earth, the peaceful throne of the Divine Being. Think, then, how quiet, how gentle and pure, how reverent, you should be.

Gerhard Tersteegen

I cannot tell you how much I love you. But that which of all things I have most at heart, with regard to you, is the real progress of your soul in the divine life. Heaven seems to be awakened in you. It is a tender plant. It requires stillness, meekness, and the unity of the heart, totally given up to the unknown workings of the Spirit of God, who will do all His work in the calm soul that has no hunger or desire except to escape out of the mire of its earthly life into its lost union and life in God. I mention this out of a fear of your giving in to an eagerness about many things, which, though seemingly innocent, yet divide and weaken the workings of the divine life within you.

William Law

And Enoch walked with God: and he was not; for God took him. —Genesis 5:24

Oh for a closer walk with God,
A calm and heavenly frame;
A light to shine upon the road
That leads me to the Lamb!

William Cowper

Is it possible for any of us in these modern days to so live that we may walk with God? Can we walk with God in the shop, in the office, in the household, and on the street? When men exasperate us, work wearies us, the children fret and the servants annoy, and our best-laid plans fall to pieces and our castles in the air are dissipated like bubbles that break at a breath, then can we walk with God? That religion which fails us in the everyday trials and experiences of life has a flaw somewhere in it. It should be more than a plank to sustain us in the rushing tide and land us exhausted and dripping on the other side. It ought, if it comes from above, to be always, day by day, to our souls as the wings of a bird, bearing us away from and beyond the impediments that seek to hold us down. If the divine love is a conscious presence, an indwelling force with us, it will do this.

Christian Union

November 1

Of whom the whole family in heaven and earth is
named. —Ephesians 3:15

One family, we dwell in Him;
    One church above, beneath;
Though now divided by the stream,
    The narrow stream of death.

One army of the living God,
    To His command we bow:
Part of His host has crossed the flood,
    And part is crossing now.

                                        Charles Wesley

Let us, then, learn that we can never be lonely or forsaken in this life. Will they forget us because they are *"made perfect"* (Heb. 12:23)? Will they love us the less because they now have power to love us more? If we do not forget them, will they not remember us with God? No trial, then, can isolate us, no sorrow can cut us off from the communion of saints. Kneel down, and you are with them. Lift up your eyes, and the heavenly world, high above all perturbation, hangs serenely overhead. Only a thin veil, it may be, floats between. All whom we loved and all who loved us, whom we still love no less while they love us yet more, are always near because they are always in His presence in whom we live and dwell.

                    Cardinal Henry Edward Manning

November 2

Wherefore seeing we also are compassed about with so great a cloud of witnesses, let us lay aside every weight, and the sin which doth so easily beset us, and let us run with patience the race that is set before us.
—Hebrews 12:1

When the powers of hell prevail
    O'er our weakness and unfitness,
Could we lift the fleshly veil,
    Could we for a moment witness
Those unnumbered hosts that stand
    Calm and bright on either hand;

Oh, what joyful hope would cheer,
    Oh, what faith serene would guide us!
Great may be the danger near,
    Greater are the friends beside us.

Anonymous

We are encircled by a cloud of witnesses whose hearts throb in sympathy with every effort and struggle, and who thrill with joy at every success. How should this thought check and rebuke every worldly feeling and unworthy purpose, and enshrine us, in the midst of a forgetful and unspiritual world, with an atmosphere of heavenly peace! They have overcome, have risen, are crowned, are glorified; but still they remain to us our assistants, our comforters. And, in every hour of darkness their voices speak to us: "So we grieved, so we struggled, so we fainted, so we doubted; but we have overcome, we have obtained, we have seen, we have found, and in our victory behold the certainty of your own."

Harriet Beecher Stowe

November 3

Wherefore putting away lying, speak every man truth with his neighbour: for we are members one of another.
—Ephesians 4:25

In conversation be sincere;
Keep conscience as the noontide clear;
Think how All-seeing God thy ways
And all thy secret thoughts surveys.

Thomas Ken

*T*he essence of lying is in deception, not in words. A lie may be told by silence, by equivocation, by the accent on a syllable, by a glance of the eye attaching a peculiar significance to a sentence. And, all these kinds of lies are worse and baser by many degrees than a lie plainly worded, so that no form of blinded conscience is so far sunk as that which comforts itself for having deceived because the deception was by gesture or silence instead of utterance.

John Ruskin

He that is accustomed to deceptions and insincere in trifles, will try in vain to be true in matters of importance, for truth is a thing of habit rather than of will. You cannot in any given case by any sudden and single effort will to be true, if the habit of your life has been insincerity.

Frederick William Robertson

A soft answer turneth away wrath: but grievous words stir up anger. —Proverbs 15:1

Doest thou well to be angry? —Jonah 4:4

Renew Thine image, Lord, in me,
Lowly and gentle may I be;
   No charms but these to Thee are dear;
No anger mayst Thou ever find,
No pride in my unruffled mind,
   But faith, and heaven-born peace be there.

Paul Gerhardt

Neither say nor do anything displeasing to your neighbor, and if you have been lacking in charity, seek his forgiveness, or speak to him with gentleness. Speak always with mildness and in a low tone of voice.

Lorenzo Scupoli

Injuries do not hurt more in the receiving than in the remembrance. A small injury will go as it comes. A great injury may dine or sup with me, but none at all will lodge with me. Why should I vex myself because another has vexed me? Grief for things past that cannot be remedied, and care for things to come that cannot be prevented, may easily hurt and can never benefit me. I will therefore commit myself to God in both and enjoy the present.

Bishop Joseph Hall

The temple of God is holy, which temple ye are.
—1 Corinthians 3:17

Now shed Thy mighty influence abroad
On souls that would their Father's image bear;
Make us as holy temples of our God,
Where dwells forever calm, adoring prayer.

Carl Johann Philipp Spitta

*T*he pearl of eternity is the church or temple of God within you, the consecrated place of divine worship, where alone you can worship God in spirit and in truth. When once you are well grounded in this inward worship, you will have learned to live unto God above time and place. For every day will be Sunday to you, and wherever you go, you will have a priest, a church, and an altar along with you. For when God has all that He should have of your heart, when you are wholly given up to the obedience of the light and spirit of God within you, to will only in His will, to love only in His love, to be wise only in His wisdom, then it is that everything you do is as a song of praise. Then the common business of your life is a conforming to God's will on earth, as angels do in heaven.

William Law

He will fulfil the desire of them that fear him: he also will hear their cry, and will save them. —Psalm 145:19

Delight thyself also in the LORD; and he shall give thee the desires of thine heart. —Psalm 37:4

Though today may not fulfill
All thy hopes, have patience still;
For perchance tomorrow's sun
Sees thy happier days begun.

Paul Gerhardt

*H*is great desire and delight is God, and by desiring and delighting, he has Him. Delight in the Lord, and He will give you your heart's desire, Himself. Then surely you will have all. Any other thing commit to Him, and He will bring it to pass.

Robert Leighton

All who call on God in true faith, earnestly from the heart, will certainly be heard and will receive what they have asked and desired, although not in the hour or in the measure or the very thing that they ask. Yet they will obtain something greater and more glorious than they had dared to ask for.

Martin Luther

November 7

I was not disobedient unto the heavenly vision.
—Acts 26:19

The LORD our God will we serve, and his voice will we obey. —Joshua 24:24

I will shun no toil or woe,
Where Thou leadest I will go,
   Be my pathway plain or rough;
If but every hour may be
Spent in work that pleases Thee,
   Ah, dear Lord, it is enough!

Gerhard Tersteegen

All these longings and doubts, and this inward distress, are the voice of the Good Shepherd in your heart, seeking to call you out of all that is contrary to His will. Oh, let me entreat of you not to turn away from His gentle pleadings.

Hannah Whitall Smith

"The fear of man bringeth a snare" (Prov. 29:25). By halting in our duty and giving back in the time of trial, our hands grow weaker and our ears grow dull as to hearing the language of the true Shepherd, so that when we look at the way of the righteous, it seems as though it was not for us to follow them.

John Woolman

November 8

Lo, I come to do thy will, O God. —Hebrews 10:9

Teach me to do thy will; for thou art my God.
—Psalm 143:10

Lo! I come with joy to do
    The Father's blessed will;
Him in outward worlds pursue,
    And serve His pleasure still.
Faithful to my Lord's commands,
    I still would choose the better part;
Serve with careful Martha's hands,
    And loving Mary's heart.

Charles Wesley

A soul cannot be regarded as truly subdued and consecrated in its will, and as having passed into union with the divine will, until it has a disposition to do promptly and faithfully all that God requires, as well as to endure patiently and thankfully all that He imposes.

Thomas Cogswell Upham

When we have learned to offer up every duty connected with our situation in life as a sacrifice to God, a settled employment becomes just a settled habit of prayer.

Thomas Erskine

Do the duty that lies nearest you, which you know to be a duty. Your second duty will already have become clearer.

Thomas Carlyle

November 9

Yet will I not forget thee. Behold, I have graven thee upon the palms of my hands; thy walls are continually before me. —Isaiah 49:15–16

Among so many, can He care?
Can special love be everywhere?
A myriad homes, a myriad ways,
And God's eye over every place?

I asked: my soul bethought of this;
In just that very place of His
Where He hath put and keepeth you,
God hath no other thing to do!

Adeline D. T. Whitney

*G*ive free and bold play to those instincts of the heart which believe that the Creator must care for the creatures He has made, and that the only real effective care for them must be that which takes each of them into His love. Knowing what He loves, He separately surrounds it with His separate sympathy. There is not one life that the Life-giver ever loses out of His sight. There is not one who sins so that He casts it away. There is not one who is not so near to Him that whatever touches this person touches Him with sorrow or with joy.

Phillips Brooks

In him we live, and move, and have our being.
—Acts 17:28

*Whither shall I go from thy spirit? or whither shall I
flee from thy presence?* —Psalm 139:7

Yea! In Thy life our little lives are ended,
    Into Thy depths our trembling spirits fall;
In Thee enfolded, gathered, comprehended,
    As holds the sea her waves—Thou hold'st us all.
                      Eliza Scudder

W here then is our God? You say, "He is every-where"; then show me anywhere that you have met Him. You declare Him everlasting; then tell me any moment that He has been with you. You believe Him ready to help those who are tempted and to lift those who are bowed down; then in what passionate hour did you subside into His calm grace? In what sorrow did you lose yourself in His *"more exceeding"* (2 Cor. 4:17) joy? These are the testing questions by which we may learn whether we, too, have raised our altar to an *"unknown God"* (Acts 17:23) and pay the worship of the blind, or whether we commune with Him in whom *"we live, and move, and have our being."*

                      James Martineau

Walk worthy of the Lord unto all pleasing, being fruitful in every good work, and increasing in the knowledge of God; strengthened with all might, according to his glorious power, unto all patience and longsuffering with joyfulness. —Colossians 1:10–11

To be the thing we seem,
To do the thing we deem
    Enjoined by duty;
To walk in faith, nor dream
Of questioning God's scheme
    Of truth and beauty.

Anonymous

*T*o shape the whole future is not our problem, but only to shape faithfully a small part of it, according to rules already known. It is perhaps possible for each of us, who will ask with due earnestness, to ascertain clearly what he, for his own part, ought to do. This let him, with true heart, do and continue doing. The general issue will, as it has always done, rest well with a higher intelligence than ours. This day you know ten commanded duties. You see in your mind ten things that should be done for the one that you actually do! *Do* one of them. This of itself will show you ten others that can and will be done.

Thomas Carlyle

November 12

I must work the works of him that sent me, while it is day: the night cometh, when no man can work.
—John 9:4

Wherefore have ye not fulfilled your task? —Exodus 5:14

He who intermits
The appointed task and duties of the day
Untunes full oft the pleasures of the day;
Checking the finer spirits that refuse
To flow, when purposes are lightly changed.

William Wordsworth

By putting off things beyond their proper times, one duty treads upon the heels of another, and all duties are felt as irksome obligations. They are a yoke beneath which we fret and lose our peace. In most cases the consequence of this is that we have no time to do the work as it ought to be done. It is therefore done rashly, with eagerness, with a greater desire simply to get it done than to do it well and with very little thought of God throughout.

Frederick William Faber

Sufficient for each day is the good thereof, equally as the evil. (See Matthew 6:34.) We must do at once, and with our might, the merciful deeds that our hands find to do, else they will never be done, for our hands will find other tasks, and the undone deeds will fall through. Every unconsummated good feeling, every unfulfilled purpose that His spirit has prompted, will one day charge us as faithless and disloyal before God.

John Hamilton Thom

November 13

Blessed is the man whom thou chastenest, O LORD, and teachest him out of thy law. —Psalm 94:12

Truly this is a grief, and I must bear it.
—Jeremiah 10:19

Hold in thy murmurs, heaven arraigning!
The patient see God's loving face;
Who bear their burdens uncomplaining,
'T is they that win the Father's grace.

Anonymous

*D*o not run to this and that for comfort when you are in trouble, but bear it. Be uncomfortably quiet. Be uneasily silent. Be patiently unhappy.

James Pierrepoint Greaves

Hard words will disturb. Unkindness will pierce. Neglect will wound. Threatened evils will make the soul quiver. Sharp pain or weariness will rack the body, or make it restless. But what did the psalmist say? "When my heart is vexed, I will complain." (See Psalm 102:1.) To whom? Not of God, but to God.

Edward B. Pusey

Surely, I have thought, I do not want to have a grief that would not be a grief. I feel that I will be able to take up my cross in a religious spirit soon, and then it will be all right.

James Hinton

November 14

Thou art my servant: I have formed thee; thou art my servant: O Israel, thou shalt not be forgotten of me.
—Isaiah 44:21

Oh, give Thy servant patience to be still,
    And bear Thy will;
Courage to venture wholly on the arm
    That will not harm;
The wisdom that will never let me stray
    Out of my way;
The love, that, now afflicting, knoweth best
    When I should rest.

                John Mason Neale

*A*ccept His will entirely, and never suppose that you could serve Him better in any other way. You can never serve Him well, save in the way He chooses. Supposing that you were never to be set free from such trials, what would you do? You would say to God, "I am Yours. If my trials are acceptable to You, give me more and more." I have full confidence that this is what you would say, and then you would not think more of it. At any rate, you would not be anxious. Well, do the same now. Make friends with your trials, as though you were always to live together, and you will see that when you cease to take thought for your own deliverance, God will take thought for you. And, when you cease to help yourself eagerly, He will help you.

                Francis de Sales

Ah, if you knew what peace there is in an accepted sorrow!

              Madame Jeanne Guyon

Fear thou not; for I am with thee: be not dismayed; for I am thy God: I will strengthen thee; yea, I will help thee; yea, I will uphold thee with the right hand of my righteousness. —Isaiah 41:10

Lord, be Thou near and cheer my lonely way;
With Thy sweet peace my aching bosom fill;
Scatter my cares and fears; my griefs allay,
And be it mine each day
To love and please Thee still.

Pierre Corneille

*W*hat if the wicked nature, which is as a sea casting out mire and dirt, rage against you? There is a river, a sweet, quiet, flowing river, the streams of which will make glad your heart (Ps. 46:4). Learn in quietness and stillness to retire to the Lord, and wait upon Him, in whom you will feel peace and joy in the midst of your trouble from the cruel and vexing spirit of this world. So, wait to know your work and service to the Lord every day, in your place and station. And the Lord will make you faithful in them, and you will lack neither help, support, nor comfort.

Isaac Penington

Thou wilt keep him in perfect peace, whose mind is stayed on thee: because he trusteth in thee. —Isaiah 26:3

What comforts, Lord, to those are given,
Who seek in Thee their home and rest!
They find on earth an opening heaven,
And in Thy peace are amply blest.

Wolfgang Christoph Dessler

God is a tranquil being and abides in a tranquil eternity. So must your spirit become a tranquil and clear little pool, in which the serene light of God can be mirrored. Therefore, shun all that is disquieting and distracting, both within and without. Nothing in the whole world is worth the loss of your peace. Even the faults that you have committed should only humble but not disquiet you. God is full of joy, peace, and happiness. Endeavor then to obtain a continually joyful and peaceful spirit. Avoid all anxious care, vexation, murmuring, and melancholy, which darken your soul and render you unfit for the friendship of God. If you do perceive such feelings arising, turn gently away from them.

Gerhard Tersteegen

Every day will I bless thee; and I will praise thy name for ever and ever. —Psalm 145:2

Commit thy works unto the LORD, and thy thoughts shall be established. —Proverbs 16:3

Lord, I my vows to Thee renew;
Disperse my sins as morning dew;
Guard my first springs of thought and will,
And with Thyself my spirit fill.

Thomas Ken

*M*orning by morning think, for a few moments, of the chief employments of the day. Think of any one thing of greater importance than others, your own especial trial, any occasions of it which are likely to come that day, and by one short strong act commend yourself beforehand in all to God. Offer all your thoughts, words, and deeds to Him, to be governed, guided, and accepted by Him. Choose some great occasions of the day that bring with them the most trial to you, on which, above others, to commend yourself to God.

Edward B. Pusey

Will you not, before venturing away from your early quiet hour, *"commit thy works"* to Him definitely, the special things you have to do today, and the unforeseen work that He may add in the course of it?

Frances Ridley Havergal

Hereby know we that we dwell in him, and he in us, because he hath given us of his Spirit. —1 John 4:13

> Within! Within, oh turn
> Thy spirit's eyes, and learn
> Thy wandering senses gently to control;
> Thy dearest Friend dwells deep within thy soul,
>   And asks thyself of thee,
> That heart, and mind, and sense, He may make whole
>   In perfect harmony.

Gerhard Tersteegen

*W*ait patiently, trust humbly, depend only upon, seek solely a God of light and love, of mercy and goodness, of glory and majesty, ever dwelling in the inmost depth and spirit of your soul. There you have all the secret, hidden, invisible Upholder of all the creation. It is He whose blessed operation will always be found by a humble, faithful, loving, calm, patient introversion of your heart to Him. It is He who has within you His hidden heaven, which will open itself to you as soon as your heart is left wholly to His eternal, ever-speaking Word and ever-sanctifying Spirit within you. Beware of all eagerness and activity of your own natural spirit and temper. Do not run in any hasty ways of your own. Be patient under the sense of your own vanity and weakness, and patiently wait for God to do His own work, and in His own way.

William Law

November 19

If any man among you seem to be religious, and bridleth not his tongue, but deceiveth his own heart, this man's religion is vain. —James 1:26

I said, I will take heed to my ways, that I sin not with my tongue. —Psalm 39:1

No sinful word, nor deed of wrong,
    Nor thoughts that idly rove;
But simple truth be on our tongue,
    And in our hearts be love.

                    St. Ambrose

Let us all resolve, first, to attain the grace of silence. Second, let us determine to deem all fault-finding that does no good a sin, and to resolve when we are happy ourselves not to poison the atmosphere for our neighbors by calling on them to remark every painful and disagreeable feature of their daily lives. Third, let us practice the grace and virtue of praise.

              Harriet Beecher Stowe

Surrounded by those who constantly exhibit defects of character and conduct, we will mar our own peace without having the satisfaction of benefiting others, if we yield to a complaining and impatient spirit.

              Thomas Cogswell Upham

*Ye have need of patience, that, after ye have done the
will of God, ye might receive the promise.*
—Hebrews 10:36

Sweet Patience, come:
Not from a low and earthly source,
Waiting, till things shall have their course,
Not as accepting present pain
In hope of some hereafter gain,
Not in a dull and sullen calm,
But as a breath of heavenly balm,
Bidding my weary heart submit
To bear whatever God sees fit:
Sweet Patience, come!
Hymns of the Church Militant

*P*atience endues her scholars with contentment of mind and evenness of temper, preventing all repining grumbling and impatient desires and inordinate affections. Disappointments here are no crosses, and all anxious thoughts are disarmed of their sting. In her habitations dwell quietness, submission, and long-suffering. All fierce, turbulent inclinations are hereby allayed. The eyes of the patient fixedly wait on the inward power of God's providence, and they are thereby mightily enabled towards their salvation and preservation.

Thomas Tryon

*Man shall not live by bread alone, but by every word
that proceedeth out of the mouth of God.* —Matthew 4:4

*A man's life consisteth not in the abundance of the
things which he possesseth.* —Luke 12:15

Whate'er God does is well,
Whether He gives or takes!
And what we from His hand receive
    Suffices us to live.
He takes and gives, while yet He loves us still.
    Then love His will.

Benjamin Schmolcke

*I*s that beast better, that has two or three mountains to graze on, than a little bee that feeds on dew or manna and lives upon what falls every morning from the storehouse of heaven, clouds, and providence?

Jeremy Taylor

For myself, I am certain that the good of human life cannot lie in the possession of things that for one man to possess is for the rest to lose. Rather, it lies in things that all can possess alike, and where one man's wealth promotes his neighbor's.

Benedict Spinoza

Every situation is happy to a person who bears it with tranquillity.

Boëthius

Your Father knoweth what things ye have need of.
—Matthew 6:8

Seek ye first the kingdom of God, and his righteousness; and all these things shall be added unto you.
—Matthew 6:33

Thy kingdom come, with power and grace,
    To every heart of man;
Thy peace, and joy, and righteousness
    In all our bosoms reign.

Charles Wesley

*G*od bids us, then, by past mercies, by present graces, by fears of becoming ill, by hopes in His goodness, earnestly to seek Him and His righteousness with our whole hearts. And, all these things, all you need for soul and body, peace, comfort, joy, the overflowing of His consolations, will be added over and above to you.

Edward B. Pusey

Grant us, O Lord, we beseech You, always to seek Your kingdom and righteousness. And of whatever You see us to stand in need, mercifully grant us an abundant portion. Amen.

Be content to be a child, and let the Father proportion out daily to you what light, what power, what exercises, what circumstances, what fears, what troubles He sees fit for you.

Isaac Penington

*I have taught thee in the way of wisdom; I have led thee
in right paths.* —Proverbs 4:11

> We know not what the path may be
>   As yet by us untrod;
> But we can trust our all to Thee,
>   Our Father and our God.
>
> William Josiah Irons

*W*e have very little command over the circumstances in which we may be called by God to bear our part. We have unlimited command over the temper of our souls, but next to no command over the outward forms of trial. The most energetic will cannot order the events by which our spirits are to be periled and tested. Powers quite beyond our reach—death, accident, fortune, another's sin—may change in a moment all the conditions of our lives. With tomorrow's sun, existence may have new and awful aspects for any of us.

John Hamilton Thom

Oh, my friend, do not look out at what stands in the way. What if it looks dreadfully as a lion? Is not the Lord stronger than any obstacle? But look in, where the law of life is written, and the will of the Lord revealed, so that you may know what the Lord's will is concerning you.

Isaac Penington

Be of good courage, and he shall strengthen your heart,
all ye that hope in the LORD. —Psalm 31:24

Let not your heart be troubled, neither let it be afraid.
—John 14:27

In heavenly love abiding,
No change my heart shall fear;
And safe is such confiding,
For nothing changes here.
Anna Laetitia Waring

A true Christian, who has power over his own will, may live nobly and happily and enjoy a clear heaven within the serenity of his own mind perpetually. When the sea of this world is roughest and most tempestuous about him, then can he ride safely at anchor within the haven by a sweet compliance of his will with God's will. He can look about him, and with an even and indifferent mind behold the world either to smile or frown upon him. Also, he will not abate in the least his contentment for all the ill and unkind usage he meets with in this life. He who has mastery over his own will, feels no violence from without, finds no contests within. When God calls him out of this state of mortality, he finds in himself a power to lay down his own life, and it is not so much taken from him, as quietly and freely surrendered up by him.

Dr. John Smith

And the LORD, he it is that doth go before thee; he will be with thee, he will not fail thee, neither forsake thee: fear not, neither be dismayed. —Deuteronomy 31:8

Know well, my soul, God's hand controls
Whate'er thou fearest;
Round Him in calmest music rolls
Whate'er thou hearest.

John Greenleaf Whittier

*T*he lessons of the moral sentiment are, once for all, an emancipation from the anxiety that takes the joy out of all life. It teaches a great peace. It comes itself from the highest place. It is that which, being in all sound natures and strongest in the best and most gifted men, we know to be implanted by the Creator of men. It is a commandment at every moment and in every condition of life to do the duty of that moment and to abstain from doing the wrong.

Ralph Waldo Emerson

Go face the fire at sea, or the cholera in your friend's house, or the burglar in your own, or what danger lies in the way of duty, knowing you are guarded by the cherubim of Destiny.

Ralph Waldo Emerson

*Behold, I am with thee, and will keep thee in all places
whither thou goest.* —Genesis 28:15

Be quiet, soul:
Why shouldst thou care and sadness borrow,
Why sit in nameless fear and sorrow,
The livelong day?
God will mark out thy path tomorrow
In His best way.

Anonymous

I had hoped, Madame, to find you here and was
rejoicing in that hope, but God has sent you
elsewhere. The best place is wherever He puts us,
and any other would be undesirable, all the worse
because it would please our fancy and would be of
our own choice. Do not think about distant events.
This uneasiness about the future is unwholesome
for you. We must leave to God all that depends on
Him and think only of being faithful in all that depends upon ourselves. When God takes away that
which He has given you, He knows well how to re-
place it, either through other means or by Himself.

Fénelon

The LORD hath been mindful of us: he will bless us.
—Psalm 115:12

My Father! What am I, that all
Thy mercies sweet like sunlight fall
    So constant o'er my way?
That Thy great love should shelter me,
And guide my steps so tenderly
    Through every changing day?

Anonymous

What a strength and spring of life, what hope and trust, what glad, unresting energy, is in this one thought—to serve Him who is "my Lord." He is ever near me, ever looking on, seeing my intentions before He beholds my failures, knowing my desires before He sees my faults. He is encouraging me to endeavor greater things, and yet accepting the least; inviting my poor service, and yet, above all, content with my poorer love. Let us try to realize this, whatever, wherever we are. The humblest and the simplest, the weakest and the most encumbered, may love Him not less than the busiest and strongest, the most gifted and laborious. If our hearts are clear before Him, if He is to us our chief and sovereign choice, dear above all, and beyond all desired, then all else matters little. That which concerns us He will perfect in stillness and in power.

Cardinal Henry Edward Manning

*Yea, I have loved thee with an everlasting love: therefore
with lovingkindness have I drawn thee.*
—Jeremiah 31:3

On the great love of God I lean,
Love of the Infinite, Unseen,
With nought of heaven or earth between.
This God is mine, and I am His;
His love is all I need of bliss.

Horatius Bonar

If ever human love was tender and self-sacrificing and devoted, then infinitely more is divine love tender and self-sacrificing and devoted. If ever human love could bear and forbear, then infinitely more is divine love glad to bear and forbear. If ever human love could suffer gladly for its loved ones, if ever it was willing to pour itself out in a lavish abandonment for the comfort or pleasure of its objects, then infinitely more is divine love to suffer and to lavish its best of gifts and blessings upon the objects of its love. Put together all the most tender love you know of, the deepest you have ever felt and the strongest that has ever been poured out upon you. Heap upon it all the love of all the loving human hearts in the world. Then multiply it by infinity, and you will begin, perhaps, to have some faint glimpse of what the love of God is.

Hannah Whitall Smith

My sons, be not now negligent: for the LORD hath chosen you to stand before him, to serve him.
—2 Chronicles 29:11

Bright be my prospect as I pass along;
An ardent service at the cost of all,
Love by untiring ministry made strong,
And ready for the first, the softest call.
Anna Laetitia Waring

*T*here are many things that appear to be trifles, which greatly tend to weaken the soul and hinder its progress in the path to virtue and glory. The habit of indulging in things that our judgment cannot thoroughly approve, grows stronger and stronger by every act of self-gratification, and we are led on by degrees to an excess of luxury that must greatly weaken our hands in the spiritual warfare. If we do not endeavor to do that which is right in every particular circumstance, though trifling, we will be in great danger of letting the same negligence take place in matters more essential.

Margaret Woods

The will can only be made submissive by frequent self-denials, which must keep in subjection its outbursts and inclinations. Great weakness is often produced by indulgences that seem of no importance.

Miguel Molinos

*Why art thou cast down, O my soul? and why art thou
disquieted in me? hope thou in God: for I shall yet
praise him for the help of his countenance.*
—Psalm 42:5

We are troubled on every side, yet not distressed.
—2 Corinthians 4:8

> Oh, my soul, why art thou vexed?
>   Let things go e'en as they will;
> Though to thee they seem perplexed,
>   Yet His order they fulfill.

A. H. Francke

*T*he vexation, restlessness, and impatience that
small trials cause, arise wholly from our igno-
rance and lack of self-control. We may be thwarted
and troubled, it is true, but these things put us into
a condition for exercising patience, and meek submission, and the self-abnegation in which alone the
fullness of God is to be found.

Gaston Jean Baptiste, Baron de Renty

Every day deny yourself some satisfaction,
bearing all the inconveniences of life, for the love of
God: cold, hunger, restless nights, ill health, unwel-
come news, the faults of others, contempt, ingratitude of friends, malice of enemies, calumnies, our
own failings, lowness of spirits, the struggle in overcoming our corruptions. Bear all these with patience
and resignation to the will of God. Do all this as
unto God, with the greatest privacy.

Bishop Thomas Wilson

December 1

Charity envieth not;...thinketh no evil.
—1 Corinthians 13:4–5

Why dost thou judge thy brother? or why dost thou set at nought thy brother? —Romans 14:10

He that despiseth his neighbour sinneth.
—Proverbs 14:21

Look thou with pity on a brother's fall,
But dwell not with stern anger on his fault;
The grace of God alone holds thee, holds all;
Were that withdrawn, thou too wouldst swerve and halt.
James Edmeston

*I*f, on hearing of the fall of a brother, however differing or severed from us, we feel the least inclination to linger over it instead of hiding it in grief and shame or veiling it in the love that covers a multitude of sins, let us be very watchful. We should also be careful if, in seeing a joy or a grace or an effective service given to others, we do not rejoice, but feel depressed. The most diabolical of passions may mask itself as humility or zeal for the glory of God.

Elizabeth Charles

Love takes up no malign elements. Its spirit prompts it to cover in mercy all things that ought not to be exposed, to believe all of good that can be believed, to hope all things that a good God makes possible, and to endure all things so that the hope may be made good.

John Hamilton Thom

December 2

Therefore thou art inexcusable, O man, whosoever thou art that judgest: for wherein thou judgest another, thou condemnest thyself; for thou that judgest doest the same things. —Romans 2:1

> Search thine own heart. What paineth thee
> In others, in thyself may be;
> All dust is frail, all flesh is weak;
> Be thou the true man thou dost seek.
>
> John Greenleaf Whittier

A saint's life in one man may be less than common honesty in another. From us, whose consciences He has reached and enlightened, God may look for a martyr's truth, a Christian's unworldly simplicity, before He will place us on a level even with average people. We perhaps think our lives are at least harmless. We do not consider what He may think of them, when compared with the invitations of His that we have slighted, with the aims of His Providence we are leaving without our help, with the glory for ourselves we are refusing and casting away, and with the vast sum of blessed work that daily faithfulness in time can raise without overwork on any single day.

John Hamilton Thom

December 3

Now the God of hope fill you with all joy and peace in believing, that ye may abound in hope, through the power of the Holy Ghost. —Romans 15:13

To heaven I lift my waiting eyes;
There all my hopes are laid;
The Lord that built the earth and skies
Is my perpetual aid.

Isaac Watts

*D*o not grovel in things below, among earthly cares, pleasures, anxieties, toils, if you would have a good strong hope on high. Lift up your cares with your heart to God, if you would hope in Him. Then see what in you is most displeasing to God. This is what holds your hope down. Strike firmly, repeatedly, in the might of God, until it gives way. Your hope will soar at once with your thanks to God who delivers you.

Edward B. Pusey

The snares of the Enemy will be so known to you and discerned, the way of help will be so manifest and easy, that the snares will be broken. The poor entangled bird will fly away singing from the nets and entanglements of the hunter. Praises will spring up, and great love in your heart, to the Forgiver and Redeemer.

Isaac Penington

December 4

*Fight the good fight of faith, lay hold on eternal life,
whereunto thou art also called.* —1 Timothy 6:12

Oh, dream no more of quiet life;
Care finds the careless out; more wise to vow
Thy heart entire to faith's pure strife;
So peace will come, thou knowest not when or how.

Lyra Apostolica

Who are you who complains of your life of toil?
Do not complain. Look up, my wearied
brother. See your fellow workmen there in God's
eternity, surviving there, they alone surviving, sacred band of the immortals, celestial bodyguard of
the empire of mankind. To you, heaven is not unkind, though it may be severe. Heaven is kind, as a
noble mother, as that Spartan mother, saying while
she gave her son his shield, "With it, my son, or
upon it." You too will return home in honor, to your
far-distant home in honor. Do not doubt it, if in the
battle you keep your shield! You, in the eternities
and deepest death-kingdoms, are not an alien. You
are a citizen everywhere. Do not complain.

Thomas Carlyle

December 5

The God of all grace, who hath called us unto his eternal glory by Christ Jesus, after that ye have suffered a while, make you perfect, stablish, strengthen, settle you.
—1 Peter 5:10

Take heed, and be quiet; fear not, neither be faint-hearted. —Isaiah 7:4

How shalt thou bear the cross that now
So dread a weight appears?
Keep quietly to God, and think
Upon the Eternal Years.
Frederick William Faber

*G*od forgive them who raise an ill report upon the sweet cross of Christ. It is but our weak and dim eyes, which look but to the black side, that make us mistake. Those who can take that difficult tree handsomely upon their backs and fasten it on prudently will find it such a burden as wings to a bird, or sails to a ship.

Samuel Rutherford

Blessed is any weight, however overwhelming, which God has been so good as to fasten with His own hand upon our shoulders.
Frederick William Faber

We cannot say this or that trouble will not befall, yet we may, by help of the Spirit, say, Nothing that does befall will make me do that which is unworthy of a Christian.

Richard Sibbes

December 6

This God is our God for ever and ever: he will be our guide even unto death. —Psalm 48:14

For the LORD shall be thy confidence. —Proverbs 3:26

> Be still, my soul! Thy God doth undertake
> To guide the future, as He has the past:
> Thy hope, thy confidence, let nothing shake,
> All now mysterious shall be bright at last.
> Jane Borthwick

He has kept and folded us from ten thousand ills when we did not know it. In the midst of our security we should have perished every hour, except that He sheltered us from *"the terror by night;* [and from] *the arrow that flieth by day"* (Ps. 91:5), from the powers of evil that walk in darkness, from snares of our own evil will. He has kept us even against ourselves and saved us even from our own undoing. Let us read the traces of His hand in all our ways, in all the events, the chances, the changes of this troubled state. It is He who folds and feeds us, who makes us to go in and out, to be faint or to find pasture, to lie down by the still waters or to walk by the way that is parched and forsaken.

Cardinal Henry Edward Manning

We are never without help. We have no right to say of any good work, It is too hard for me to do; or of any sorrow, It is too hard for me to bear; or of any sinful habit, It is too hard for me to overcome.

Elizabeth Charles

December 7

Acquaint now thyself with him, and be at peace.
—Job 22:21

*All thy children shall be taught of the LORD; and great
shall be the peace of thy children.* —Isaiah 54:13

Unite, my roving thoughts, unite
In silence soft and sweet;
And thou, my soul, sit gently down
At thy great Sovereign's feet.

Philip Doddridge

Yes! Blessed are those holy hours in which the
soul retires from the world to be alone with
God. God's voice, as Himself, is everywhere. Within
and without, He speaks to our souls if we would
hear. Only the din of the world, or the tumult of our
own hearts, deafens our inward ear to it. Learn to
commune with Him in stillness, and He, whom you
have sought in stillness, will be with you when you
go abroad.

Edward B. Pusey

The great step and direct path to the fear and
awe-inspiring reverence of God, is to meditate and,
with a sedate and silent hush, to turn the eyes of
the mind inward. It is there to seek, and with a
submissive spirit wait, at the gates of Wisdom's
temple. Then the divine voice and distinguishing
power will arise in the light and center of a man's
self.

Thomas Tryon

Blessed be the God and Father of our Lord Jesus Christ, who hath blessed us with all spiritual blessings.
—Ephesians 1:3

As sorrowful, yet alway rejoicing. —2 Corinthians 6:10

> It is not happiness I seek,
> Its name I hardly dare to speak;
> It is not made for man or earth,
> And Heaven alone can give it birth.
>
> There is a something sweet and pure,
> Through life, through death it may endure;
> With steady foot I onward press,
> And long to win that Blessedness.
>
> Louisa Jane Hall

*T*he elements of *happiness* in this present life no man can command, even if he could command himself, for they depend on the action of many wills, on the purity of many hearts. By the highest law of God, the holiest must always bear the sins and sorrows of the rest. But over the *blessedness* of his own spirit, circumstance need have no control. God has in this given an unlimited power to the means of preservation, of grace and growth, at every man's command.

John Hamilton Thom

There is in man a higher purpose than love of happiness. He can do without happiness and instead find blessedness!

Thomas Carlyle

December 9

For this shall every one that is godly pray unto thee in a time when thou mayest be found: surely in the floods of great waters they shall not come nigh unto him.
—Psalm 32:6

Be not o'ermastered by thy pain,
    But cling to God, thou shalt not fall;
The floods sweep over thee in vain,
    Thou yet shalt rise above them all;
For when thy trial seems too hard to bear,
Lo! God, thy King, hath granted all thy prayer:
        Be thou content.

Paul Gerhardt

It is the Lord's mercy to give you breathings after life and cries unto Him against that which oppresses you. Happy will you be when He will fill your soul with that which He has given you to breathe after. Do not be troubled if troubles abound and there are tossing and storms and tempests and no peace or anything visible left to support. Yet, lie still, and sink beneath, until a secret hope stirs. This hope will stay the heart in the midst of all these, until the Lord administers comfort. He knows how and what relief to give to the weary traveler who does not know where it is or which way to look or where to expect a path.

Isaac Penington

December 10

Behold, we count them happy which endure.
—James 5:11

If ye endure chastening, God dealeth with you as with sons. —Hebrews 12:7

Trials must and will befall;
But with humble faith to see
Love inscribed upon them all,
This is happiness to me.

William Cowper

*D*o not be afraid of those trials that God may see fit to send upon you. It is with the wind and storm of tribulation that God separates the true wheat from the chaff. Always remember, therefore, that God comes to you in your sorrows, as really as in your joys. He lays low, and He builds up. You will find yourself far from perfection if you do not find God in everything.

Miguel Molinos

God has provided a sweet and quiet life for his children, if they could improve and use it. He has provided a calm and firm conviction in all the storms and troubles that are about them, however things go, to find content, and to be careful for nothing.

Robert Leighton

Oh that thou wouldest bless me indeed, and enlarge my coast, and that thine hand might be with me, and that thou wouldest keep me from evil, that it may not grieve me! —1 Chronicles 4:10

Ye shall serve the LORD your God, and he shall bless thy bread, and thy water. —Exodus 23:25

What I possess, or what I crave,
    Brings no content, great God, to me,
If what I would, or what I have,
    Be not possest, and blest, in Thee;
    What I enjoy, O make it mine,
    In making me that have it, Thine.

John Quarles

Offer up to God all pure affections, desires, regrets, and all the bonds that link you to home, kindred, and friends, together with all your works, purposes, and labors. These things, which are not only lawful, but also sacred, become then the matter of thanksgiving and offering. Memories, plans for the future, wishes, intentions; works just begun, half done, all but completed; emotions, sympathies, affections—all these things throng tumultuously and dangerously in the heart and will. The only way to master them is to offer them up to Him as once yours under Him, but always His by right.

Cardinal Henry Edward Manning

I delight to do thy will, O my God: yea, thy law is within my heart. —Psalm 40:8

A patient, a victorious mind,
That life and all things casts behind,
    Springs forth obedient to Thy call;
A heart that no desire can move,
But still to adore; believe, and love,
    Give me, my Lord, my Life, my All.

Paul Gerhardt

That piety which sanctifies us and which is a true devotion to God, consists in doing all His will precisely at the time, in the situation, and under the circumstances in which He has placed us. Perfect devotedness requires not only that we do the will of God, but also that we do it with love. God would have us serve Him with delight. It is our hearts that He asks of us.

Fénelon

Devotion is really neither more nor less than a general inclination and readiness to do that which we know to be acceptable to God. It is that *"free spirit"* (Ps. 51:12), of which David spoke when he said, *"I will run the way of thy commandments, when thou shalt* [set my heart at liberty]" (Ps. 119:32). People of ordinary goodness walk in God's way, but the devout run in it. At length they almost fly in it. To be truly devout, we must not only do God's will, but we must also do it cheerfully.

Francis de Sales

December 13

*So teach us to number our days, that we may apply our
hearts unto wisdom.* —Psalm 90:12

*Seek not ye what ye shall eat, or what ye shall drink,
neither be ye of doubtful mind.* —Luke 12:29

> Our days are numbered: let us spare
> Our anxious hearts needless care:
> 'T is Thine to number out our days;
> 'T is ours to give them to Thy praise.
>
> Madame Jeanne Guyon

Every day let us renew the consecration to God's service. Every day let us, in His strength, pledge ourselves afresh to do His will, even in the most real trifle, and to turn aside from anything that may displease Him. He does not bid us to bear the burdens of tomorrow, next week, or next year. Every day we are to come to Him in simple obedience and faith, asking help to keep us and aid us through that day's work. And, tomorrow and tomorrow and tomorrow, through years of long tomorrows, it will be but the same thing to do, leaving the future always in God's hands, sure that He can care for it better than we. Blessed trust can thus confidingly say, "This hour is mine with its present duty. The next is God's, and when it comes, His presence will come with it."

Anonymous

And as many as walk according to this rule, peace be on them, and mercy, and upon the Israel of God.
—Galatians 6:16

Lord, I have given my life to Thee,
And every day and hour is Thine,
What Thou appointest let them be;
Thy will is better, Lord, than mine.

Anna B. Warner

*B*egin at once. Before you venture away from this quiet moment, ask your King to take you wholly into His service and place all the hours of this day quite simply at His disposal. Ask Him to make and keep you ready to do just exactly what He appoints. Never mind about tomorrow. One day at a time is enough. Try it today, and see if it is not a day of strange, almost curious peace, so sweet that you will be only too thankful, when tomorrow comes, to ask Him to take it also. It will become a blessed habit to hold yourself simply and *"wholly at thy commandment" "for any manner of service"* (1 Chron. 28:21). The *"any manner"* is not necessarily active work. It may be waiting—whether half an hour or half a lifetime—learning, suffering, or sitting still. But will we be less ready for these, if any of them are His appointments for today? Let us ask Him to prepare us for all that He is preparing for us.

Frances Ridley Havergal

December 15

Return unto thy rest, O my soul; for the LORD hath dealt bountifully with thee. —Psalm 116:7

We which have believed do enter into rest. —Hebrews 4:3

Rest is not quitting
    The busy career;
Rest is the fitting
    Of self to its sphere.

'T is loving and serving
    The highest and best!
'T is onwards, unswerving,—
    And that is true rest.

John Sullivan Dwight

As a result of her strong faith, the inner life of Catherine of Genoa was characterized in a remarkable degree by what may be termed rest, or quietude, which is only another form or expression for true interior peace. It was not, however, the quietude of a lazy inaction, but the quietude of an inward acquiescence. It was not a quietude that feels nothing and does nothing, but that higher and divine quietude which exists by feeling and acting in the time and degree of God's appointment and God's will. It was a principle in her conduct to give herself to God in the discharge of duty, and to leave all results without anxiety in His hands.

Thomas Cogswell Upham

December 16

Thou understandest my thought afar off. —Psalm 139:2

Who can understand his errors? cleanse thou me from secret faults. —Psalm 19:12

My newest griefs to Thee are old;
    My last transgression of Thy law,
Though wrapped in thought's most secret fold,
    Thine eyes with pitying sadness saw.
Harriet McEwen Kimball

Lord our God, great, eternal, wonderful in glory, You who keep covenant and promises for those who love You with their whole hearts, who are the Life of all, the Help of those who flee unto You, the Hope of those who cry unto You, cleanse us from our sins, secret and open, and from every thought displeasing to Your goodness. Cleanse our bodies and souls, our hearts and consciences, that with a pure heart and a clear soul, with perfect love and calm hope, we may venture confidently and fearlessly to pray unto You. Amen.
Coptic Liturgy of St. Basil

The dominion of any sinful habit will fearfully estrange us from His presence. A single consenting act of inward disobedience in thought or will is enough to let a cloud fall between Him and us, and to leave our hearts cheerless and dark.
Cardinal Henry Edward Manning

December 17

The fruit of the Spirit is love, joy, peace, longsuffering,
gentleness, goodness, faith, meekness, temperance.
 —Galatians 5:22–23

Herein is my Father glorified, that ye bear much fruit;
so shall ye be my disciples. —John 15:8

O Breath from out the Eternal Silence! blow
    Softly upon our spirits' barren ground;
The precious fulness of our God bestow,
    That fruits of faith, love, reverence may abound.
                    Gerhard Tersteegen

*I*s it possible we should be ignorant whether we feel tempers contrary to love or not? Whether we rejoice always, or are burdened and bowed down with sorrow? Whether we have a praying or a dead, lifeless spirit? Whether we can praise God and be resigned in all trials, or feel murmurings, fretfulness, and impatience under them? Is it not easy to know if we feel anger at provocations or whether we feel our tempers mild, gentle, peaceable, and easy to be entreated, or feel stubbornness, self-will, and pride? Whether we have slavish fears or are possessed of that perfect love which casts out all fear?

                    Hester Ann Rogers

December 18

We trust in the living God. —1 Timothy 4:10

Thy secret judgment's depth profound
Still sings the silent night;
The day, upon his golden round,
Thy pity infinite.

Isaac Williams
Translated from Latin

Now that I no longer have any sense for the transitory and perishable, the universe appears transformed before my eyes. The dead, heavy mass that did but stop up space has vanished, and in its place there flows onward, with the rushing music of mighty waves, an eternal stream of life and power and action, which issues from the original source of all life—from Your life, O Infinite One! For all life is Your life, and only the religious eye penetrates to the realm of true beauty.

Johann Gottlieb Fichte

What is nature? Is it not the living garment of God? O heavens, is it He who ever speaks through you, who lives and loves in you, who lives and loves in me? Sweeter than dayspring to the shipwrecked in Nova Zembla; like the mother's voice to her little child who strays, bewildered, weeping, in unknown tumults; like soft streamings of celestial music to my too-exasperated heart, came that Evangel. The universe is not dead and demonic, a charnel house with ghosts, but godlike, and my Father's.

Thomas Carlyle

O LORD, be gracious unto us; we have waited for thee.
—Isaiah 33:2

And now, Lord, what wait I for? my hope is in thee.
—Psalm 39:7

He never comes too late;
    He knoweth what is best;
Vex not thyself in vain;
    Until He cometh, rest.

B. T.

We make mistakes, or what we call such. The nature that could fall into such mistake exactly needs, and in the goodness of the dear God is given, the living of it out. And beyond this, I believe more: that in the pure and patient living out of it we come to find that we have fallen, not into hopeless confusion of our own wild, ignorant making, but that the finger of God has been at work among our lines. We emerge into His blessed order. He is forever making for us our own undoings, and He makes them beforehand. He evermore restores our souls.

A. D. T. Whitney

The Lord knows how to make stepping-stones for us of even our defects. It is what He lets them be for. He remembers—He remembered in the making—that we are but dust, the dust of earth out of which He chose to make something a little lower than the angels.

A. D. T. Whitney

Take no thought how or what ye shall speak: for it shall be given you in that same hour what ye shall speak.
—Matthew 10:19

> Just to follow hour by hour
> As He leadeth;
> Just to draw the moment's power
> As it needeth.
>
> Frances Ridley Havergal

You have a disagreeable duty to do at twelve o'clock. Do not blacken nine and ten and eleven, and all between, with the color of twelve. Do the work of each, and reap your reward in peace. So when the dreaded moment in the future becomes the present, you will meet it walking in the light, and that light will overcome its darkness. The best preparation is the present well seen to, the last duty done. For this will keep the eye so clear and the body so full of light that the right action will be perceived at once. The right words will rush from the heart to the lips. And the man, full of the Spirit of God because he cares for nothing but the will of God, will trample on the evil thing in love. He will be sent, it may be, in a chariot of fire to the presence of his Father, or stand unmoved amid the cruel mockings of the men he loves.

George MacDonald

Hast thou not known? hast thou not heard, that the everlasting God, the LORD, the Creator of the ends of the earth, fainteth not, neither is weary?...He giveth power to the faint; and to them that have no might he increaseth strength. —Isaiah 40:28–29

> Workmen of God! oh, lose not heart,
> But learn what God is like;
> And in the darkest battlefield
> Thou shalt know where to strike.
>
> Frederick William Faber

*F*or the rest, let that vain struggle to read the mystery of the Infinite cease to harass us. It is a mystery that, through all ages, we will only read a line of here and there. Do we not already know that the name of the Infinite is Good, is God? Here on earth we are as soldiers, fighting in a foreign land, who do not understand the plan of the campaign and have no need to understand it, seeing well what is at our hand to be done. Let us do it like soldiers, with submission, with courage, with a heroic joy. Behind us, behind each one of us, lie six thousand years of human effort, human conquest. Before us is the boundless time, with its as yet uncreated and unconquered continents and El Dorados that we, even we, have to conquer, to create. From the bosom of Eternity there shines for us celestial guiding stars.

Thomas Carlyle

I will wait upon the LORD, that hideth his face from the house of Jacob, and I will look for him. —Isaiah 8:17

What heart can comprehend Thy name,
  Or, searching, find Thee out?
Who art within, a quickening flame,
  A presence round about.

Yet though I know Thee but in part,
  I ask not, Lord, for more:
Enough for me to know Thou art,
  To love Thee and adore.

Frederick L. Hosmer

Stand up, O heart, and do not yield one inch of your rightful territory to the usurping intellect. Hold fast to God in spite of logic, and yet not quite blindly. Do not be torn from your grasp upon the skirts of His garments by any wrench of atheistic hypothesis that seeks only to hurl you into utter darkness. But do not refuse to let your hands be gently unclasped by that loving and pious philosophy that seeks to draw you from the feet of God only to place you in His bosom. Trustfully, though tremblingly, let go of the robe, and you will rest upon the heart and clasp the very living soul of God.

James Hinton

Thou therefore endure hardness, as a good soldier of Jesus Christ. —2 Timothy 2:3

> Where our Captain bids us go,
> 'T is not ours to murmur, "No."
>   He that gives the sword and shield,
>   Chooses too the battlefield
> On which we are to fight the foe.

Anonymous

Of nothing may we be more sure than this: that, if we cannot sanctify our present situation, we could sanctify no other. Our heaven and our almighty Father are there or nowhere. The obstructions of that situation are given for us to heave away by the concurrent touch of a holy spirit and labor of strenuous will. Its gloom is given for us to tint with some celestial light. Its mysteries are for our worship. Its sorrows are for our trust. Its perils are for our courage. Its temptations are for our faith. Soldiers of the cross, it is not for us, but for our Leader and our Lord, to choose the field. It is ours, taking the station that He assigns, to make it the field of truth and honor, though it is the field of death.

James Martineau

*Giving thanks unto the Father, which hath made us
meet to be partakers of the inheritance of the saints in
light.* —Colossians 1:12

The souls most precious to us here
    May from this home have fled;
But still we make one household dear;
    One Lord is still our head.
Midst cherubim and seraphim
    They mind their Lord's affairs;
Oh! if we bring our work to Him
    Our work is one with theirs.

                  Thomas Hornblower Gill

*W*e are apt to feel as if nothing we could do on earth bears a relation to what the good are doing in a higher world, but it is not so. Heaven and earth are not so far apart. Every disinterested act, every sacrifice to duty, every exertion for the good of *"one of the least of* [Christ's] *brethren"* (Matt. 25:40), every new insight into God's works, every new impulse given to the love of truth and goodness, associates us with the departed, brings us nearer to them, and is as truly heavenly as if we were acting, not on earth, but in heaven. The spiritual tie between us and the departed is not felt as it should be. Our union with them daily grows stronger, if we daily make progress in what they are growing in.

                  William Ellery Channing

*That ye, being rooted and grounded in love, may be able
to comprehend with all saints what is the breadth, and
length, and depth, and height; and to know the love of
Christ, which passeth knowledge, that ye might be filled
with all the fulness of God.* —Ephesians 3:17–19

O love that passeth knowledge, thee I need;
    Pour in the heavenly sunshine; fill my heart;
Scatter the cloud, the doubting, and the dread,
    The joy unspeakable to me impart.

                        Horatius Bonar

*T*o examine its evidence is not to know Christianity, to admire its martyrs is not to know
Christianity, to compare and estimate its teachers is
not to know Christianity, to attend its rites and
services with more than Muhammadan punctuality
is not to know Christianity. But for one week, for
one day, to have lived in the pure atmosphere of
faith and love to God, of tenderness to man, is to
start to know Christianity. To have beheld earth
annihilated, and heaven opened to the prophetic
gaze of hope; to have seen evermore revealed behind
the complicated troubles of this strange, mysterious
life, the unchanged smile of an eternal Friend, and
everything that is difficult to reason solved by that
reposing trust which is higher and better than reason—to have known and felt this, I will not say for a
life, but for a single blessed hour, that, indeed, is to
have experienced Christianity.

                William Archer Butler

*The peace of God, which passeth all understanding,
shall keep your hearts and minds through Christ Jesus.*
—Philippians 4:7

Let the peace of God rule in your hearts.
—Colossians 3:15

> Drop Thy still dews of quietness,
>   Till all our strivings cease;
> Take from our souls the strain and stress,
> And let our ordered lives confess
>   The beauty of Thy peace.

John Greenleaf Whittier

*T*hese things write we unto you, that your joy may
be full" (1 John 1:4). What is fullness of joy but
peace? Joy is tumultuous only when it is not full, but
peace is the privilege of those who are *"filled with the
knowledge of the glory of the LORD"* (Hab. 2:14).
*"Thou wilt keep him in perfect peace, whose mind is
stayed on thee"* (Isa. 26:3). It is peace, springing from
trust and innocence, and then overflowing in love
towards all around him. He who is anxious thinks of
himself, is suspicious of danger, speaks hurriedly, and
has no time for the interests of others. He who lives
in peace is at rest wherever his lot is cast.

Cardinal John Henry Newman

Through the spirit of divine love let the violent,
obstinate powers of your nature lie stilled, the hardness of your affections softened, and your self-will
subdued. When anything contrary stirs within you,
sink into the blessed ocean of meekness and love.

Gerhard Tersteegen

Wherefore thou art no more a servant, but a son; and if a son, then an heir of God through Christ.
—Galatians 4:7

Nor by the terrors of a slave
God's sons perform His will,
But with the noblest powers they have
His sweet commands fulfil.

Isaac Watts

Our thoughts, good or bad, are not in our command, but every one of us has at all hours duties to do. These he can do negligently like a slave or faithfully like a true servant. Do the duty that is nearest you—that first, and that well. All the rest will disclose themselves with increasing clarity and make their successive demands. If your duties are ever so small, I advise you, set yourself with double and triple energy and punctuality to do them hour after hour, day after day.

Thomas Carlyle

Whatever we are—high or lowly, learned or unlearned, married or single, in a full house or alone, charged with many affairs or dwelling in quietness—we have our daily round of work, our duties of affection, obedience, love, mercy, industry, and the like. And, that which makes one man to differ from another is not so much what things he does, as his manner of doing them.

Cardinal Henry Edward Manning

Now the God of peace...make you perfect in every good work to do his will, working in you that which is well-pleasing in his sight. —Hebrews 13:20–21

Be ready to every good work. —Titus 3:1

So, firm in steadfast hope, in thought secure,
    In full accord to all Thy world of joy,
May I be nerved to labors high and pure,
    And Thou Thy child to do Thy work employ.
John Sterling

*B*e with God in your outward works. Refer them to Him. Offer them to Him. Seek to do them in Him and for Him. He will be with you in them, and they will not hinder, but rather invite, His presence in your soul. Seek to see Him in all things, and in all things He will come close to you.
Edward B. Pusey

Nothing less than the majesty of God, and the powers of the world to come, can maintain the peace and sanctity of our homes, the order and serenity of our minds, the spirit of patience and tender mercy in our hearts. Then will even the merest drudgery of duty cease to humble us, when we transfigure it by the glory of our own spirits.
James Martineau

Finally, brethren, whatsoever things are true, whatsoever things are honest, whatsoever things are just, whatsoever things are pure, whatsoever things are lovely...think on these things. —Philippians 4:8

As he thinketh in his heart, so is he. —Proverbs 23:7

> Still may Thy sweet mercy spread
> A shady arm above my head,
> About my paths; so shall I find
> The fair center of my mind
> Thy temple, and those lovely walls
> Bright ever with a beam that falls
> Fresh from the pure glance of Thine eye,
> Lighting to eternity.
>
> Richard Crashaw

*M*ake yourselves nests of pleasant thoughts. None of us yet know, for none of us have been taught in early youth, what fairy palaces we may build of beautiful thoughts, as proof against all adversity. We may build bright, satisfied memories, noble histories, faithful sayings, treasure-houses of precious and restful thoughts, which care cannot disturb, pain make gloomy, or poverty take away from us. They are houses built without hands, for our souls to live in.

John Ruskin

A man has no freer or quieter place to which he may retire than into his own soul, particularly when he has within him such thoughts that by looking into them he is immediately in perfect tranquillity. And I affirm that tranquillity is nothing else than the good ordering of the mind.

Marcus Aurelius Antoninus

December 30

O LORD, I know that the way of man is not in himself:
it is not in man that walketh to direct his steps.
                    —Jeremiah 10:23

I will direct all his ways. —Isaiah 45:13

Come, Light serene and still!
Our darkened spirits fill
    With thy clear day:
Guide of the feeble sight,
Star of grief's darkest night,
Reveal the path of right,
    Show us Thy way.

                    Robert II of France

*T*here had been solemn appointed seasons in Anna's life when she was accustomed to enter upon a full and deliberate survey of her business in this world. The claims of each relationship, and the results of each occupation, were then examined in the light of eternity. It was then, too, that her fervent prayer to be enabled to discern the will of God far more perfectly was examined, not only in the indications given of it for her guidance through each day's occupations, but as it might concern duties not yet brought home to her conscience, and therefore unprovided for in her life.

                    Anna, or *Passages from Home Life*

December 31

Forgetting those things which are behind, and reaching forth unto those things which are before, I press toward the mark for the prize of the high calling of God in Christ Jesus. —Philippians 3:13–14

> Yet I argue not
> Against Heaven's hand or will, nor bate a jot
> Of heart or hope; but still bear up and steer
> Right onward.
>
> John Milton

It is not by regretting what is irreparable that true work is to be done, but by making the best of what we are. It is not by complaining that we do not have the right tools, but by using well the tools we have. What we are, and where we are, is God's providential arrangement—God's doing, though it may be man's misdoing—and the manly and the wise way is to look your disadvantages in the face and see what can be made out of them. Life, like war, is a series of mistakes, and he is not the best Christian nor the best general who makes the fewest false steps. He is the best who wins the most splendid victories by the retrieval of mistakes. Forget mistakes. Organize victory out of mistakes.

Frederick William Robertson